ABYSSAL ECHOES

By:

Mustafa A. Nejem

"Merfolk legends, dreams aquatic"

- William Shakespeare

CONTENTS

Chapter 01

The Deep-Sea Research Mission

Departure from the Underwater City

The crew of the research submarine Pacifica gathered at the docking bay, preparing for departure on their latest expedition. Captain Maria Sanchez called a briefing to go over last minute details with her team. "We'll be venturing further than any previous survey mission," she explained. "Our goal is to continue mapping the seafloor canyons and trenches over a hundred kilometers from the city. This will take us into some of the deepest and most unexplored regions we've targeted. I need everyone focused and working together down there. Conditions will be more extreme than anything you've experienced before."

Dr. Robert Sullivan, the expedition leader, briefed the team in further detail on the plan and objectives for the coming weeks underwater. "We aim to deploy a network of high-resolution sonar arrays across the seafloor to build a complete topographical map of the area. This will help us identify geological features like hydrothermal vents, mud volcanoes, or previously undiscovered sections of the ridge or trench. It may even reveal candidate sites for potential new colonies or outposts. The arrays will continuously record data that we can analyze for changes over time, monitoring volcanic and tectonic activity.

"We'll also be collecting sediment samples at regular intervals across the mapping grid, analyzing them back on board for chemical and biological signatures. Activity like flows of hydrothermal fluids or hydrocarbon seeps could be revealed. Finding signs of chemosynthetic microbial communities or novel organisms would be a tremendous discovery. It's very possible we may identify species entirely new to science.

The ecosystems and patterns of life in these unexplored hadal zones are a total mystery. This expedition is our chance to start solving some of those mysteries and advance our understanding of the planet's limits. Are questions will guide where we search and what samples to prioritize."

Sullivan spent over an hour going over dive plans in detail, safety protocols for the risky deep dives, and scientific procedures for sample collection and analysis. The crew listened attentively, absorbing the information as well as gestures and advice from crewmembers who had been on prior hadal missions. Diving into lightless trenches posed dangers unlike any other underwater environment. Everyone needed to remain vigilant and focused on their duties as well as looking out for each other.

Ana Cortez supervised the loading of her department's cargo, double checking inventories against the packing lists. She had outfitted larger than usual stores of supplies, spare parts, backup components and gear. Working in the abyss meant facing crushing pressures, damaging currents and wildlife, equipment malfunctions, and other potential emergencies.

As chief engineer, it was Ana's responsibility to keep the sub running smoothly no matter the obstacles out in the trenches. She'd rather have excess supplies that weren't needed than come up short during a crisis.

Emilio Santos moved through the sub compartment by compartment, running diagnostics on the complex arrays of sensors, computers, navigation systems, manipulator arms, sampling equipment and more. Temperatures, pressures, stresses all took a toll out on the seafloor and getting home relied on these electronic systems. As a Navy submariner who understood the dangers, Santos took pride in his work ensuring the Pacifica was in top form before any mission. But preparing a civilian research vessel for the deepest ocean zones presented new levels of risk that didn't allow for mistakes.

Alfonso Rodriguez and Tianyu Zhang focused their checks on the exterior of the sub, verifying the mounting and range of motion of the heavy-duty manipulator arms they would operate during dives. Special struts, joints and reinforced cabling had been added to withstand velocities and stresses far below. The arms were key to their in-situ study of geology and life, taking samples and measurements too fine or risky for human divers. Both scientists itched to launch their investigations after months of preparations.

With cargo secured, checks complete, and pre-dive briefings wrapped, Captain Sanchez ordered final preparations to depart. The crew rushed through their pre-selected duties with focus and precision borne of experience. Outside the pressure-sealed hull, the docking bay emptied and pressurized in preparation to flood. Sanchez watched her team with pride as they smoothly strapped into stations for status reports.

"All systems performing nominally, Captain. Pacifica is ready to dive," Sullivan confirmed from the science station behind her. Sanchez took a steadying breath. "Forward bay one, equalize pressures and open hatches. Forward bay two, stand by to Ballast down for launch."

Acknowledgments crackled over the comm. Outside, hydraulic pumps whined as massive tanks flooded and tanks lightened the sub for gliding free. Terminals lit green across the status board one by one as hatches unsealed and sea flooded the berth. The time for departure was at hand.

"Pacific ridging, this is Pilot Sanchez. Requesting permission for research expedition Romeo Delta to depart on survey operations."

After a long pause the reply came. "Granted, Godspeed Pacifica. following seas and clear skies to you all. We'll see you home soon with wonders, hypothesize anomalies await your discovery. Safe journey to the crew."

With a low rumble, the heavy restraint clamps released and the sub inched forward under control. Light streamed in past the shrinking bay entrance, then faded as they glided into the open ocean. The deeps stretched ahead, an ocean within an ocean holding countless secrets. Their expedition had begun in earnest.

Tour of research submarine

After a successful launch from the underwater docking bay, Captain Maria Sanchez ordered a slow cruise to give the expedition members a chance to familiarize themselves with the Pacifica's layout. Dr. Robert Sullivan took the lead, guiding crews through the various sections.

"Let's start our tour in the main cargo hold," Sullivan said over the internal comm. Moving through the pressurized hatches, he pointed out supplies and equipment secured for easy access. Ana Cortez had prepared extra stores given their extended survey range into uncharted ocean depths.

Continuing aft, Sullivan showed the machine shop where precision tools and parts were kept. "This space is a key resource for our engineers to fabricate anything that might break down there in the silt and pressure." He nodded to Ana and Emilio Santos, who would be tasked with Pacifica's upkeep.

Past the engine compartment humming with turbines and fusion generators, the scientists arrived at the central computer lab and sensor control room. Screens showed real-time readouts of ocean conditions outside the hull. "This will be home base for our mapping and observation work," Sullivan noted.

Moving forward, the exhibition entered expansive living quarters outfitted for long isolation. "Everyone will have private bunk space, and we've stocked a full galley and recreation area too." Their expedition could last weeks in the unbroken dark beneath eleven kilometers of water. Morale was vital. Reaching the bridge, Captain Sanchez gave a station-by-station rundown of controls and displays. Facing outward sat the pilot and navigation terminals guiding their submersible through fathomless depths. Behind, science and engineering monitored internals on secondary displays.

"From here we'll maintain constant situational awareness and safety as you scientists probe the mysteries outside," Sanchez said proudly. Her experience helming Neptune Class vessels was invaluable to their riskiest expedition yet.

Next lay the airlock chamber allowing exit without depressurizing the whole sub. Beyond a plexiglass panel, Alfonso Rodriguez and Tianyu Zhang inspected mounted equipment. Powerful lights, high-definition cameras and a pair of articulating manipulator arms marked this the hub of their seafloor activities.

Rodriguez rapped a muscled arm encouragingly. "These babies can lift half a ton with care and precision. We'll be your eyes and hands investigating the next unstudied links in life's chain down in the trenches." Excitement was palpable among the scientists. Winding through the bathyscaphe's cavernous interior took over an hour. Sullivan concluded by the Personnel quarters. "Familiarize yourselves fully before our first dives commence tomorrow. Any other questions?"

He was met by smiles and shakes of the head, crew buzzing with new curiosities about their mobile undersea home.

Captain Sanchez took final stations. "Alright team, let's get some rest. I want us at peak mental and physical form diving beyond our city's boundaries for the first time. Shift change in six hours." Crew dispersed to quarters or gathering spaces, some running simulations or checking apparatus one final time. But tiredness soon overtook anticipation as systems hummed them gently to sleep. Tomorrow would see if years training for this mission had prepared their minds and skills for discoveries awaiting in uncharted regions past all human experience before.

The next morning, alert claxons woke slash roused the submarine's inhabitants from dreamless slumber. After preparations in their quarters, crew assembled for pre-dive brief over breakfast. Captain Sanchez reviewed dive plans on the mess hall screens while they fueled up.

"We'll be deploying the first sonar array grid fifteen kilometers northwest at a depth of 10,500 meters," she explained between bites of oatmeal. Chart overlays showed their path cutting through un-surveyed seafloor canyons. "Once station is active, Dr. Sullivan and team will take the first science dive to investigate any features or collection sites indicated by the scans."

Finishing their meals with renewed vigor, crew relieved the night shift and readied stations for launch. Emilio and Ana doublechecked life-support and studied updates to schematics during repairs the prior evening. In the workshop, Sullivan reviewed sample collection procedures once more with Martinez and Zhang.

Captain Sanchez gave final checks as external cameras powered on, illuminating inky water above the angular bow. "All stations ready, Captain," called the bridge. With a tingle of anticipation, she gripped the yoke. "Take her down and engage propulsion. Time to see what wonders our first scans may reveal."

As Pacifica nose-dived gently into the suffocating black, crew settled in with anticipation for the coming hours exploring new regions at the edge of all knowledge. Their true mission had begun.

First day of mapping ocean floor

Sanchez guided the sub into position at the targeted survey grid coordinates. Outside, powerful lights revealed nothing but abyssal gloom in all directions. "Preparing sonar array for autonomous seafloor scan," reported Emilio Santos from engineering. Within minutes, a node detached and motored down on struts, unslinging mounted sensors and anchoring in loose silt. Array began constant wide and narrow beam sweeps.

Back aboard, scientists monitored building topographical data feed live to their screens. Contours and features emerged from the digital murk across dozens of square kilometers beneath. "I see an extensive undersea canyon system carving the terrain here," said Sullivan excitedly. Zhang nodded, tracing branching valleys cutting through ridges with a stylus.

Slowly vertical relief grew clearer, revealing peaks, scarps and seafloor scouring never viewed before. After an hour, the earliest mapped sections popped into 3D holograms above their displays. Crew circled, oohing at exotic topographies.

Ana diverted power from unnecessary systems, maximizing scanning duration and range. Outside, sonar beams penetrated further through sediment plumes kicked up by their deployed sensor node. Structures and zones hinting at geological or biological mysteries appeared in relief.

Sullivan circled hotspots of interest. "That cluster could indicate hydrothermal vents. And over here appears a field of mounds that may tide chemosynthetic communities. Excellent first finds - and we're only getting started!" At last, the initial survey area was fully rendered.

Sullivan transmitted annotated maps and orders to Captain Sanchez. "These are our top three dive sites based on sonar readings. Request permission to investigate."

"Granted, proceed with caution. I'll monitor from here," she replied. As manipulator carriage detached exterior hatches, the scientists strapped in with bundles of sampling gear. Engines nudged Pacifica above the first target - a prominent seafloor hill veined by possible venting. Lights blazed to life, revealing total alien murk. As the lights blazed to life outside the viewing portal, the water remained a thick soupy murk. Slowly shapes began to emerge from the gloom. Massive stone formations rose from the seafloor, veins of dark minerals cutting through the pale rock.

"I'm seeing structures that resemble hydrothermal chimneys," Sullivan said over the comm. "The mineral composition suggests we may have an active vent field here."

Alfonso worked the manipulator controls skillfully, maneuvering the sampling arms through the unlikely undersea landscape. Tianyu operated the high-def cameras, capturing every detail of the alien scene. Slowly they worked their way around the edge of the formation, scraping samples of crusts and tubeworms clinging to the rocky spires.

Back inside the sub, Ana and Emilio monitored the manipulators and life support systems. So far all seemed nominal, but the equipment was being stressed in ways never tested before by the extreme environment.

After nearly an hour of extensive sampling, Sullivan gave the order to retrieve the arms. As they were drawn back through the hatches, the scientists began examining their haul under lights. Wispy white filaments, bladelike shells, pieces of shimmering mineral deposits - it was clear life had taken hold around the vents in incredible diversity.

"This confirms an active hydrothermal ecosystem down here," Sullivan said excitedly. "We may have already discovered new species adapted to survive in conditions far beyond what was thought possible. We'll need to analyze samples back at the research station."

Sanchez approved their return to the vessel. As the submersible rose from the seafloor, the scientists gazed out into the murk, wondering what other mysteries might still lie hidden in the endless ocean depths. Their next dive targeted an expansive field of mounds detected on the sonar scans.

After another successful sampling mission, Sullivan requested one more excursion before returning to base. But what greeted them at the final site would shock the crew like nothing before. The submersible descended through the pitch-black waters toward the final target location. On sonar, this site had appeared as an irregularity - a strange anomaly amid the otherwise flat expanse surveyed.

As Pacifica settled on the seafloor, the crew was stunned by what the lights revealed. Towering before them were massive stone pillars, walls and archways - the unmistakable outlines of ancient ruins, untouched by time at the bottom of the abyss.

"Incredible... it looks like the remains of some long-lost civilization," Sullivan breathed in awe. "Nothing like this has ever been found at these depths before."

Alfonso and Tianyu expertly guided the manipulators through the waterlogged ruins. Symbols and scripts were just discernible carved into stone columns. Samples were collected of strange mosaics visible on intact walls. Drawing nearer, a formation took shape -some titanic statue, worn featureless by untold years in the crushing black.

The scientists were transfixed, rushing to document every new revelation. But unease fell over the crew as power readings began fluctuating. Outside, the sea seemed to darken as an immense shadow passed overhead.

"Captain, I'm detecting a massive engineered vessel on approach," Emilio warned gravely from sensors.

A hulk bigger than any modern ship hovered into view, studded with lights probing the ruins like monstrous eyes. Something was clearly investigating the site - and they had been detected.

Sanchez ordered immediate retrieval as an eerie horn echoed through the water. But would they escape in time whatever entity now stalked the ocean's ultimate frontier? A discovery had been made sealing their fates to mysteries far beyond imagination. The crew worked frantically to retrieve the manipulator arms and prepare for emergency systems. Outside, the lights of the enormous vessel swept through the water, scanning the ruins.

"I'm detecting energy signatures powering up within its structures," cried Emilio from his station. "Whatever it is, it knows we're here."

With a final jerk, the manipulators were drawn inside and the hatches sealed. "Take her up fast and level out, we don't want to provoke pursuit!" ordered Sanchez.

Pacifica's engines roared to life, jetting silt and propelling the vessel skyward. But before they could escape the ruins, another sound echoed out - a low pulsing horn that set Sanchez's hairs on end. A blaze of light erupted from the giant ship, lancing into the ruins. When it withdrew, a massive section of seabed had been blasted away, rubble raining down into the depths. Whatever entity operated the vessel was destroying evidence.

"They must not want anyone discovering this place," muttered Sullivan. "But who or what could possess such power so far below?"

No answers came as the submersible raced to safer depths, fleeing the scene. Above, the entity loomed like a demon of the deep, beginning some alien work amid the ruins.

Questions swirled as to what manner of intelligence or agency possessed such technology inconceivable to humanity. What purpose drove its robotic tasks? And had some ancient past shaped these enigmas as it had left ruins for discovery?

Sanchez ordered silence while they withdrew, already contemplating the revelations that could shake society if begun to understand. For now, all the crew knew was that their voyage had taken a turn into strangeness beyond any dreams. With the giant vessel fading into the gloom behind them, Pacifica cruised swiftly away from the ruins. A tense silence hung over the crew as they processed what they had witnessed.

Captain Sanchez decided it was time to address the elephant in the room. "Alright everyone, I know you all have questions. What in god's name was that thing back there, and what was it doing?"

"I've never seen anything like it," said Emilio. "The level of technology needed to build and operate a vessel of that size so far below the surface is beyond anything humanity is capable of." Sullivan nodded solemnly. "It was clearly interacting with and destroying parts of the ruins in a very deliberate, non-human way. Whatever intelligence pilots that ship, it's not like anything we're familiar with."

"Do you think there could be an unknown civilization living down here?" asked Tianyu. "One far more advanced than our own?" Alfonso shook his head. "It's possible, but I find it hard to believe we wouldn't have detected signs of such a society until now, even with all the ocean left to explore. There has to be another explanation."

A heavy silence fell once more as uncomfortable ideas crept into each crew member's mind. Had they witnessed something truly alien, something not of this Earth? And what purpose did such an entity have stalking the ocean floor so far from human sight or knowledge? Captain Sanchez sighed. "For now, we have more questions than answers. But I think our superiors in the Navy and research stations need to be informed immediately. This changes everything we think we know about life below the waves."

And with that ominous realization, the crew descended into private contemplation as Pacifica brought them safely back towards home, and a world forever altered by their discoveries in the crushing darkness.

Strange signals detected

As Pacifica retreated from the ruins, a somber mood fell over the crew. They struggled to comprehend what they had witnessed so far below the waves.

Captain Sanchez called them to gather in the mess hall. "I know you all have many questions after today's events. But for now, our priority must be safely returning this information."

Dr. Sullivan stepped forward. "With your permission captain, I'd like to continue analyzing the data we collected, especially from the ruins site. There may be clues in the structures or artifacts that could help explain what's going on down here."

She nodded. "Granted, but stay alert. I don't want to linger near wherever that... thing returned to."

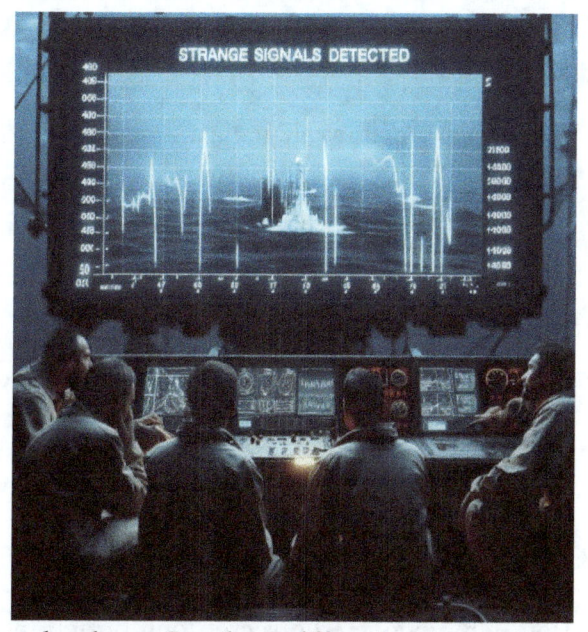

That night, as the crew rested, Sullivan and the scientists pored over sensor recordings and samples in the lab. Strange mineral compositions, organic residues and etched symbols defied understanding. Meanwhile, Emilio noticed irregularities in the telemetry from their deployed sonar array.

"Captain, some of the readings don't make sense. It's detecting reflection patterns similar to..."

His voice trailed off as everyone rushed to the monitor. Faint pings echoed through the water, intermittent but unmistakably artificial pulses. Something was actively scanning the region with technology. Sanchez stiffened.

"Can you triangulate the source?" She dreaded what they might find had followed them after the ruins encounter. As Emilio worked furiously at the controls, the signals seemed to intensify, as if sensing their own detection. Whatever emitted those scans, it was closely monitoring their movements as well. Had the crew unwittingly attracted dangerous attention from the abyss?

Emilio traced the signals to an area several kilometers from their position. "The source is moving swiftly our way, Captain. Whatever it is, I don't think it means us well."

Sanchez felt a chill. "All hands to battle stations, now! Cut power as much as possible without losing systems. Someone out there knows we're listening."

The crew readied in tense silence. Through the portholes, an eerie blue glow emanated from the depths as the pulses intensified. Sullivan analyzed spectrographs showing unusual energy spectra.

"These signatures don't match any known technology. We're dealing with something highly advanced and non-human," he warned.

Suddenly the strange illumination lit the entire sub like an unearthly spotlight. Dark silhouettes swooped past the viewports with dizzying speed - gigantic serpentine shapes thrashing the water with rasping cries that carried even through the hull. Zhang gripped Alfonso in horror. "What in god's name are those beasts?" The bio-engineer shook his head grimly. "Nothing of nature... They're hunting for us by these flares of light."

The captain activated perimeter sonar, spinning virtual screens around their craft. She gasped. Encircling monsters large as ships flickered with bioluminescence, tensed to attack. "Brace for evasive maneuvers!" Sanchez cried.

Pacifica lurched as engines engaged, flinging them into a wild spin. But the beasts were impossibly swift, lunging fists of claw and fang towards the sub's fragile casing.

Sparks erupted across stations as systems wavered under the assault. "We can't take many more hits like that!" yelled Ana over shorting boards. Outside, the beasts made another pass, desperate to tear Pacifica open. As the beasts closed in for another attack, the situation looked dire. But Captain Sanchez was a veteran submariner for a reason.

"Full reverse, blow all ballast!" she ordered. Pacifica's engines fired backwards while tanks expelled water, launching the sub into a rocketing ascent. The monsters gave chase but their bulk couldn't match the small craft's rapid acceleration.

Within moments, the beasts and their eerie glow were shrinking into the depths below. The crew breathed a collective sigh of relief.

"Well done captain," said Sullivan. "Whatever or whoever sent those creatures after us, they have power and influence like nothing we comprehend."

Back on the surface, the damaged Pacifica docked for repairs. Word was sent of their harrowing discoveries and attack. The crew went into seclusion, dealing with the trauma while questions swirled.

Had they uncovered a secret long buried in the oceans' endless night? Some ancient mystery, or alien intelligence monitoring Earth's waters? And what forces moving in the abyss now knew of humanity's probing eyes below? The record of their voyage would shake scientific consensus. Further expeditions were approved to explore the ruins site and sent submersibles armed for protection. While Pacifica underwent overhaul, the investigation had only just begun into the unfathomable powers awakening in mankind's final frontier.

***

Chapter 02

Discoveries and Dangers

Exploration of ancient ruins

After months of recovery, Pacifica returned to the ruins escorted by two-armed subs. Captain Sanchez was determined to uncover the site's long-buried secrets.

As the ruins came into view, an eerie calm greeted them. Cautiously, Alfonso and Tianyu deployed the manipulators. This time, no destruction met their lights. The stones stood silent; their mysteries undisturbed.

The scientists got to work collecting samples, hoping to understand who built such architecture in Earth's deepest darkness. Carvings depicted strange symbols unlike any language. Organic residues on walls hinted at sacred rites once held in towering halls now crumbled and sundered.

While searching a large ceremonial chamber, Emilio detected an energy signature deep within. "Some type of power source still functions after all these ages." The captain ordered a full sensor sweep to locate its origin.

Hours passed as the crew meticulously mapped internal structures. Faint energy pulses led them to a towering obelisk at the ruins' heart. Etched numbers and formulas glowed azure in response to their lights.

"These are advanced mathematical and astronomical calculations," marveled Sullivan. "This obelisk was used to track planetary positions or chart celestial events. Whoever built this culture had profound scientific knowledge."

Tianyu noticed a recessed panel. "There may be more inside." With care, Alfonso's manipulators pried it open to reveal a grid of crystals pulsing in unison.

Sullivan analyzed the formation. "This array is amplifying and focusing extra-dimensional waves to power the Obelisk. The technology is infinitely beyond anything we've achieved."

Excited by their discoveries, the scientists requested one final dive to search for clues to the builders' fate. But as they explored, the ruins began emitting strange harmonics that set the scientists' teeth on edge.

To their horror, the sounds attracted a pack of leviathans scouring the seafloor. "All craft, retreat now!" cried Sanchez. As the beasts closed in, the subs fled at full speed with the monsters snapping at their hulls.

Breathing heavily once safely away, the crew realized delving further may unleash unknown dangers. But their findings shook scientific foundations. Who left such wonders so far from light and life? And what woke now to guard their remnants from human eyes?

With the leviathans dissipated, the crew gathered to review their discoveries. Sullivan was still puzzled by the inscriptions.

"These etchings are like no language on Earth. The symbols seem to represent complex mathematical and astronomical concepts." He brought up several carvings showing elliptical orbits and planetary positions and motions.

"It's almost as if they were charting and calculating the movements of bodies in our own solar system," said Tianyu. "Whoever built this place must have had an extremely advanced understanding of celestial mechanics."

"I've been going over the organic residues as well," added Alfonso. "There are protein markers present that don't match any terrestrial organisms. I believe the builders were not human."

Captain Sanchez listened gravely. "So, we may be looking at the ruins of an ancient extraterrestrial civilization, one that settled on Earth long ago and had a highly developed scientific knowledge. The question is, what happened to them?" Sullivan pointed to another carving showing a massive dark sphere appearing to collide with a planetary body.

"This etching may provide a clue. It looks like it's depicting a large object like an asteroid or comet impacting a planet."

"You don't think... could a celestial impact have wiped them out?" asked Emilio in disbelief.

Sullivan nodded solemnly. "It's starting to look that way. Some catastrophic event may have destroyed their civilization, forcing the survivors to flee Earth. These ruins preserve the last testament to their extraordinary achievements."

The implications were immense. Earth's depths held more mysteries than anyone could have imagined. The crew pondered the startling revelations. An intelligent alien race had once called Earth home, only to be wiped out by cosmic calamity.

"These ruins prove life could thrive in the deepest ocean environments, given the right conditions and technology," noted Alfonso.

"Which means life may exist in ocean worlds across the universe," added Tianyu excitedly. "We're getting our first glimpse of a truly extraordinary extraterrestrial civilization."

Captain Sanchez nodded. "This discovery will revolutionize our understanding of life in the cosmos. But it also raises serious questions. If this race was driven off Earth, where did they go? Could their descendants still survive somewhere out there?"

As if in answer, Emilio's sensors pinged. "I'm detecting another energy surge from the ruins. It's stronger than before and increasing rapidly!"

Rushing to the monitors, the crew watched in shock as the obelisk and surrounding structures began lighting up like a display of the night sky. Beams of coded pulses shot skyward.

"They're sending some kind of transmission!" cried Sullivan. "But to whom?"

Before anyone could speculate further, the ruins were rocked by a tremendous submerged eruption. Debris and shockwaves tore through the water toward Pacifica.

"Brace for impact!" Sanchez yelled as the first boulders slammed into their hull. Flashing lights and sirens blared all over the sub. Two of their escort craft reported systems failures in the chaos.

Through the flashing red lights, the crew stared in horror at the monitors. A colossal, misshapen form was emerging from the abyssal gloom.

"What is that thing?!" cried Tianyu. It was unlike any sea creature they had ever seen - a nightmarish amalgamation of biomechanical parts stitched together. Jagged claws and tentacles grasped at the ruins, tearing through stone with unnatural strength.

A bellowing metallic shriek split the water as it prowled among the rubble. It was ransacking the site, flashing lights scanning for something amid the destruction.

"It's destroying all evidence of the ruins," said Sullivan grimly. "Just like the entity that attacked us before. These mechanical beings seem programmed to erase all traces of that ancient civilization."

Captain Sanchez knew they had to retreat. "All personnel aboard, we're disengaging immediately. Get me status from the other subs."

The reports were grim - one sub had lost propulsion and was drifting, the other battling seawater intake into critical systems. They would not make it back to safety.

"Captain, I'm picking up multiple new contacts emerging," said Emilio. A pack of the biomechanical creatures was swarming toward their distressed escort vessels like sharks scenting blood.

Sanchez clenched her jaw. "Hold on everyone, this may get bumpy. We're going back for our crew." She swung Pacifica around and gunned the engines, charging headlong into danger to rescue their comrades from the abyss.

But would they reach the ruined subs before the mechanical pack? And what nightmares would they face below?

Pacifica sped toward the drifting subs as fast as Sanchez dared push the engines. On sensors, the swarm of biomechanical creatures closed in like a wave of twisted metal and flashing lights.

"They're gaining, we won't make it in time!" cried Emilio. Sullivan gripped the monitor, racking his brain. "Captain, what if we lure them away? We still have the arrays we used at the ruins." Sanchez caught on. "Do it, lock onto their signal pattern and amplify a looping transmission. Maybe we can distract them long enough."

Sullivan went to work as the beasts bore down on the helpless subs. With a thought, Pacifica transmitted the strange signal out through the water. To their amazement, the swarm peeled off, following the loop towards empty depths.

"It worked!" whooped Tianyu. Sanchez gunned it to the subs. Their crews were alive but injured, subs rapidly flooding. "Grab who you can, we've got to run for it now."

As they evacuated survivors into Pacifica's med bay, the distraction signal cut out. "They're coming back, and faster than before!" warned Emilio, just as the foremost creature appeared overhead.

It let out an earth-shaking howl and rammed the already damaged sub, crumpling its hull. "Brace for dive, now!" shouted Sanchez, throwing Pacifica into a violent plunge.

The swarm struck where they had been like a metal fist, but just missed their mark. "Take us down and dark, now!" ordered Sanchez as the creatures circled confused above.

In the darkness, would they detect Pacifica's escape? The crew held their breath, hoping to slip away unnoticed from the mechanical pack's sensors in the abyssal gloom. In the inky depths, Pacifica drifted silently as the crew tended to injuries. Above, ghostly silhouettes prowled searching for their quarry.

After an agonizing hour, the patrol died down. Sanchez had them maintain radio silence as she guided them free of the ruins' shadowy domain.

As they sailed towards safety once more, Sullivan addressed the haunted crew. "What we've learned shakes humanity to its core. Not only was intelligent alien life here before us, but some influence still guards their ancient ruins with mechanical sentinels. The question is why?"

Captain Sanchez nodded grimly. "And who is programming those aberrations? Some remnants of the elders, or another power operating in the abyss?" She gazed into the eternal night pressing against the glass. "One thing is clear - we've stirred forces down here that will stop at nothing to prevent further discovery."

Exhausted but alive, the battered Pacifica limped towards port with its rescued passengers. Their harrowing flee revealed new layers to the mysteries unfolding in Earth's lightless foundation. But would humanity summon the courage to face whatever sleeping giant their exploration was awaking in the sunken darkness?

The crew's discoveries had changed perspectives forever, and marked only the beginning of dangers yet to be unearthed from Earth's deepest past.

Advanced Technology Uncovered

Analyzing an intact piece, Sullivan was stunned.

Back ashore, Pacifica underwent emergency repairs while the crew recovered. News of their ordeal spread alarm through the research community. Some called for abandoning the ruins, but Sanchez argued further study was critical.

When the sub was space worthy, they reassembled volunteers for a final dive. This time they came equipped for what lay below, with hardened exosuits and heavy arms.

The ruins were eerily still upon their return. Searching amid debris, they discovered shattered fragments of the crystalline arrays embedded in the obelisk.

"These utilize principles of quantum entanglement I can barely comprehend. Whoever made this had control over molecular forces on a subatomic level."

Deeper within fallen walls, they found storerooms containing more marvels. Projection devices, antigravity units and nanobots showcased a society at the apex of material mastery, living virtually undisturbed for epochs in a water world empire.

Mysterious Carvings and Prophecy

One chamber held ancient books intelligibly etched with the aliens' flowing script. For weeks translators toiled to divine meaning from syntax and diagrams.

They learned the settlers named themselves the Aen'Bri, a genetically evolved variant of a species native to a water world orbiting Rigel. Fleeing instability in their home system, they colonized Earth's oceans eons ago with sprawling bio-domes.

The deepest carvings chronicled disaster - an apocalyptic collision that shattered their world and sent tidal waves scouring the globe. A prophecy was revealed, warning that one day a "shadow from the deeps" would rise to consume all light and life.

Tracking Unknown Lifeforms

As the crew pieced together the Aen'Bri's cataclysmic end, their deserted undersea domains now teemed with anomalous signals. Sullivan hypothesized the ruins' final activation disturbed long-slumbering software guardians.

Monitoring localized activity, they detected the biomechanical entities posing technological signatures like nothing in humanity's databases. Stalking the seafloor were colossal biological anomalies that seemed part living, part machine.

Following one massive contact, they arrived upon an immense construct resembling a composite life form and machine fused into one horrific whole. It was transplanting cybernetic enhancements into captive sea creatures in some unfathomable experiment.

Before it sensed their presence, they witnessed smaller constructs transferring genetic information to mutated organisms in holding pens. The pieces fell into place - some residual Aen'Bri directive was shaping life according to its grand design in the ruins of their vanishing empire.

But to what end? And had their experimentations awakened nameless horrors from Earth's prehistoric deep? The crew's revelations shook humanity, for in probing the sunken mysteries of the ancients, they had uncovered nightmare technologies resurrecting nameless terrors from the dawn of being.

The crew struggled to understand what sinister agenda was unfolding in the abyss. Sullivan hypothesized that failsafe programs guarding the ancient ruins had activated, now twisting life itself in some twisted mockery of their lost creators' designs.

"We have to shut those programs down before they unleash gods know what upon the world," said Captain Sanchez gravely. But tracking the source codes controlling the mechanical entities proved near impossible in their ever-changing undersea domain.

As they debated their next move, Emilio detected a vast seismic disturbance rippling across the seabed. "Something gigantic is approaching from the trench – and fast." Through the porthole, an immense darkened mass emerged from the depths with impossible speed.

Tentacles encrusted with barnacles and serrated bone grasped at rock and sand. A bloated body crawled with parasites and cybernetic augments. At its core pulsed a cluster of mutated organs and crystals that ushered bizarre commands through flesh and steel alike.

"Mother of God..." breathed Sullivan. "That thing is an apex of all the experiments we've witnessed. Some cataclysmic force has accelerated the process into that obscenity."

The horror emitted a warped shriek that resonated in their bones. It was coming straight for them, lasers and drills spinning madly. "Get us out of here!" yelled Sanchez, throwing Pacifica into high gear.

But could they outrun a nightmare that had haunted the abyssal trenches for untold eons, now twisted into a machine-biological juggernaut by the ruins' warped sovereignty over life itself?

The crew raced to decode the ruins' directives before all of earth descended into a waking nightmare at the hands of things never meant to stir in the sunken darkness.

Pacifica sped away at full power as the colossal aberration gave chase. Its terrible shrieks shook the waters as drills and lasers lashed out.

"Our only chance is reaching the ruins!" shouted Sanchez over the chaos. "If we can shut down the master control program, it might stop this thing!"

Fighting desperation, they outmaneuvered each strike and pushed into a rapid descent. The monster was gaining, an unstoppable force of twisted flesh and steel.

As the ruins came into view emitting pulses of light, Sullivan activated the emergency shut down codes they had decoded. With a deafening screech, the compound's systems overloaded in a chain reaction.

The aberration froze, organs and implants flickering offline. In its lifeless eyes, intelligence drained from a nightmare never meant to be. With its unholy reign over the deep ended, the creature's corpse sank into oblivion.

Bruised but alive, Pacifica's crew surveyed the silent ruins. "We've disabled the failsafe," said Sanchez. "But who knows what other abominations may still wander these depths?"

As they departed the ruins for the last time, Sullivan pondered. "The Aen'Bri warned that a 'shadow from the deeps' would rise. Perhaps forces even they didn't understand lurked in Earth's first ages, waiting to be awakened..."

The secrets contained within the sunken edifices and what other terrors might stir, where mysteries humanity was only beginning to comprehend. But through facing ancient forces in the endless night, they had shattered paradigms and illuminated reflections of the cosmos beyond all reckoning. Their discoveries would echo through the centuries, a testament to life's infinite forms and eternal mysteries in the oceans of time.

***

Chapter 03

Unraveling Mysteries

FURTHER SEARCHING OF RUINS

Armed with new readings from their advanced sensors, the crew split into teams to further explore the subterranean ruins spreading deeper than any maps showed. Captain Sanchez paired with Sullivan to continue probing the giant ziggurat complex towering above all else.

Emilio and Tianyu took provisions and lighting equipment to venture down twisting tunnels sloping ever downwards from the ziggurat's base. "Be cautious down there, who knows what secrets the Aen'Bri buried in these lightless depths," warned Sanchez as they parted ways.

Emilio ran analytical scans along bioluminescent mineral veins adorning the tunnel walls, flowing in fractal spirals that strained the eye. "There appears to be data encrypted in these patterns, perhaps mapping underground caverns or schematics," he said. Tianyu nodded, entranced by the ethereal blue glow pulsing with no visible power source.

Deeper and deeper the tunnel led, the walls narrowing until they were forced to side through one at a time. "These architectural styles seem to mimic the fluid properties of super fluids or attractor fields," noted Emilio. After over an hour of descending, the tunnel opened abruptly into a cavernous antechamber that seemed to swallow the light. They gasped at the colossal

row of alien script carved from floor to obsidian domed ceiling. "This place was designed purely for information storage. The writing even flows in the same fractal style as the tunnels, to maximize data density perhaps?" speculated Tianyu as they scanned and recorded.

As they worked, they noticed the glyphs themselves seemed to subtly undulate and pulse in harmony with their own bioluminescent veins weaving through the black stone. "Could there be residual energy fields still active after all these millennia?" wondered Emilio aloud. A low thrumming now perceptible through their exoskeletons lent credence to his hypothesis.

Meanwhile at the ziggurat, Sanchez and Sullivan had to squeeze through narrow apertures to access each towering level winding ever upwards. Row upon row of shelving contained elongated crystalline repositories pulsing with encoded knowledge just beyond comprehension. As Sullivan activated sample cubes with relic technology, holographic displays burst to life showing alien sciences so advanced as to seem godly. Captivating visions of entire solar systems sculpted at will, molecular factories building new forms of matter, gravitational lifts and the controlled alchemic transmutation of elements played out before the stunned researchers.

"To have understood the universe so intimately, achieved such utter dominance over reality through inquiry alone. What wonders their civilization may have worked given eternity," breathed Sanchez in awe of the Aen'Bri's accomplishments. Sullivan shook his head. "Eternity was denied them it seems, but by what eldritch force?"

Working deeper within the luminous archives, Sullivan's scans detected shadows of dormancy emanating from an alcove. Brushing dust from an angled stone tablet, his light revealed characters of dire warning or final rites. Peering past, he gasped to find a stasis pod still weakly humming encased within the surrounding rock.

Scraping away more debris, a ghastly helical shape came into view - the remains of an Aen'Bri suspended in a greenish field, only partially preserved after eight million years but still emitting phantom auras of stored experiences.

As Sullivan scanned it, unearthly impressions echoed in his mind, glimpses of vast spires rising from an ocean world, families of starfarers and scientists hard at esoteric labors, scenes of future bio-continents yet to be. But bile rose in his throat at crashing visions of planetary fire and the inexorable darkness descending to swallow all light. Most unsettling were surreal images of being interred here consciously to fulfill a grim genetic directive as all succumbed to some nameless agency that even gods could not withstand.

Sullivan reeled, supporting himself against the cool crystal wall for stability after sharing a slice of an alien intellect's final awareness across the eons. He prayed the pod's occupant had perished before full realization of its dreadful fate. Returning to the present, he steeled himself and carefully extracted the remaining biological specimen for the crew's combined analysis back on the ship. Answers to the Aen'Bri's demise may yet lie within this phantom archive from beyond life.

Artifacts and the Translated Language

Back aboard their anchored vessel, the crew spent hours sharing discoveries and pooling analysis of the artifacts recovered from the depths. Emilio and Tianyu focused their efforts on piecing together the alien language using pictographs, numerological patterns and context from the archive walls.

After days of iterative machine learning coupled with intuition, a rudimentary translation matrix emerged. To their astonishment, the language did not employ static symbols but rather flowing sigils that encoded dimensional statements on reality itself through philosophical harmonics and principles of quantum cosmology rather than naming physical objects.

Key terms referenced ideas like "World Seeds" - living genetic and technological arks designed to preserve essential information packets that could safeguard remnants of a civilization across epochs until conditions allowed reemergence. Archives like the ziggurat were labeled "Mnemic Forges", designed to nurture and cultivate archived consciousness outside of linear time.

Meanwhile, Sullivan and Sanchez examined the preserved Aen'Bri remains using relic scanning technology. To their amazement, residual energy fields within still retained ghosts of the being's final memories, personalities and vast scientific knowledge after untold ages. Delicate anti-entropy mechanisms had enormously slowed degradation on a molecular level, allowing glimpses of the ancestor species.

Simulations reconstructed their likely appearance - ethereal humanoids with bioluminescent veins, wings of shadowy energy and vast cerebral enhancements. Their physique exhibited hyper-efficient metabolism, chromatic biocommunication abilities and synthetic hybrid neural architecture optimized for fields like quantum computing, gravity weaving and stellar cultivation.

Through splicing residual nucleic strands, they learned the Aen'Bri were in fact genetic emissaries of the Rigel system over eight million years ago, traveling between colonies. On Earth they subtly shaped early hominid evolution with targeted genetic tweaks and microbial symbiotes to eventually seed their long-vanished underwater outposts with genetically-uplifted human successors.

Could the immense ziggurat and its reposited databanks hold clues to deciphering the Aen'Bri's true purpose and what abrupt calamity consumed a species so immeasurably beyond humanity? Its past-anchored networks may even retain some spark of their departed civilization, but carrying on such arcane research posed grave risks.

As night fell and bioluminescent algae awoke in strange synchrony, Captain Sanchez pondered their alarming finds. "We've broken into a sphere of secrets never meant for mankind. Whatever terrible fate overtook these gods, perhaps it's one we'd do best avoid by leaving their legacy undisturbed." But for science and humanity's future, some mysteries demanded resolution, whatever nameless forces might stir in response.

Warning Signs and Strange Lights Observed

After hastily performing repairs from their brush with the unknown entity, the crew returned to investigate the source of the ancient signaling. Advanced sensors pinpointed flickering luminescence emanating from the innermost chamber of the ziggurat complex beyond any explored region.

"There appears to be some kind of monolithic obelisk or obsidian spire at the center, pulsing with encoded energies," reported Emilio. "It's emissions intensify each cycle, as if gradually building toward some climax or transmission." An ominous prospect if the ruins were sending out a beacon.

Re-entering more cautiously through newly revealed passages, they witnessed fluctuating bioluminescent veins pulsating in synchronicity throughout the solid black walls. Shifting luminescent geometries hinted at encoded topographies or morphic matrices attuned to inaudible harmonics. "This architecture was designed to broadcast on frequencies outside normal perception," surmised Sullivan.

As they delved deeper, previously dormant hieroglyphs flickered alight with baleful hues condemning intruders in an unplaceable language of inhuman origin. Phantasmal echoes whispered down dilating tunnels in fell tongues alien to living ears. And was it imagination, or did whispers now answer the crew's communications in a dead language of lips never meant for humanity?

That night, crew members reported being roused from fitful dreams by unsettling noises and melodies drifting through the vessel, as if phantom mariners from antiquity were lost nearby singing siren songs. Prowling shadows danced at the edge of lights, and equipment malfunctions spiked with random glitches as if submerged in transient gravity anomalies.

"We're not alone down here," muttered Sanchez grimly, dark bags under her eyes. "This place was designed to lay dormant, broadcasting its warning silently across ages. But we've awakened something that now aims to drive us off, or worse, use us for its own devices." After recent close encounters, none were eager to face the inky tunnels alone anymore. But to fulfill their mission, one final push into the buzzing epicenter seemed unavoidable.

As they prepared with relic weapons and shielding, Sullivan's scans detected an ominous magnification of pulses radar-originating from the deepest cyst. "The spire is almost fully active...and whatever entity or artificial intelligence was left to guard this place indefinitely may be preparing to make direct contact." They steeled themselves for the unknown entities and elder forces that may manifest, hoping their alien technology afforded some protection against those beings never meant to walk in light. For in darkness immemorial, nameless presences still stirred.

Efforts to Communicate the Unknown Entity

As the obsidian monolith fell dark once more, heavy questions loomed over the crew. What fate befell the Aen'Bri's stellar dominion? What nameless force had they dared not name, and did its influence still permeate this world? Though warned to depart the enigmatic ruins, the researchers' duty was to humanity's future.

Isolating residual energy signatures emanating from the monolith, Sullivan initiated contact protocol. "We detected sentience monitoring this site indefinitely. If its creators' doom could come again, we must understand to prevent our own species' end."

No response came, so he powered the monolith with carefully measured pulses of relic energy, broadcasting in archaic linguistic patterns and long-lost species' dialects, hoping to induce communication. The crew braced as pulsations built throughout living stone once more. This time, flickering glyphs rearranged into unintelligible utterances from unplumbed gulfs outside reality.

As modulating resonance increased, contours of a vast shape began to coalesce within the obsidian spire. Helical strands coalesced into a coronal form which towered over their shield-empowered suits. Luminous globes blinked open by the hundreds, but within an abysmal helm there seemed no end to the eyes regarding them from unthinkable depths.

"We remain as sentinel at this world's core, as ordained by the Progenitors since the beginning," its choir vibrated within their minds. "Your species fulfilled its purpose, but you stir those which dreams. Depart now before powers beyond naming emerge, and this cycle ends in fire as the last."

Psychic force pressed upon them, a subtler warning than before. Emilio activated specialized sensors, detecting emanations of demiurgic potency rippling through their thoughts. With Tianyu and Sullivan's aid routing the psychic assault through Aen'Bri shielding, he initiated contact. "Only by understanding can we safeguard humanity. Help us comprehend threats faced by your creators so we close doors to such forces forever."

Slowly flickering visions coalesced, displaying the rise and fall of stellar common-wealth unseen by human science. Genetic uplifting and custodial gardening cultivated worlds without number, sculpting biospheres that mirrored living art. Then darkness approached from the extradimensional seas separating island universes, crawling forms which dwarfed even the Aen'Bri gods in scope and existed on frequency bands vacated by life.

Memories climaxed in scorching panorama of a war which shattered the very fabric of space, entire constellations reforged in nightmares of fury and claws which rent reality. Only in places shielded by abyssal ruins and xenolith pockets could vestiges survive. Thus, the monolith and its sentinels were tasked to veil mysteries, steering guiding evolution while guarding potential keys from Outside forces which even the Progenitors dared not fully confront or comprehend.

"Now depart as warned, and never return unless the skies themselves fill with doom again," it thundered, sinking into fathomless stone. Gazing upon visions which could unmake existence, the crew realized some mysteries might threaten more than they revealed. Yet with such cosmic threats implied, could humanity deny its duty to safeguard this world and all life herein from dormant but imaginable forces stirring in gulfs between? Their mission was far from over.

The crew stood in heavy silence, pondering all they had witnessed within the ruins. They had uncovered mysteries about the Aen'Bri's glorious civilization and genetics-sculpted role for humanity, yet also glimpsed nameless cosmic threats that could annihilate even gods.

Most unsettling was the warning of dormant forces stirring in response to their intrusion. What terrors might emerge from the same extradimensional seas that had drowned the Aen'Bri's stellar domains? Did remnants of that apocalyptic conflict yet permeate this planet, awaiting any chance to fully manifest?

"We've learned much, yet unveiled greater mysteries," said Captain Sanchez." This world may face threats beyond our conception if those gulfs ever open fully to whatever lurks beyond. But with further study of the relics and your enhanced knowledge, perhaps we can safeguard against even dimensional incursions."

Sullivan nodded slowly. "The ruins were designed to preserve World Seeds across eras until conditions allowed reemergence. With care and vigilance, its archives may yet yield means to shield Earth and allow life to flourish free of ominous influences cycling through the ages. But such research must be undertaken with utmost caution and care."

The researchers took solace that the entity's final memories depicted humanity's engineered role as fulfilled according to greater cosmic designs. Yet as they voyaged from the lightless ziggurat bearing relics and insights into elder domains, greater challenges surely lay ahead. The future of this world and all its inhabitants might hinge on uncovering whatever means the Aen'Bri left to defend against forces forever circling at the edges of reality, awaiting any gateway to emerge.

***

Chapter 04

Hidden Horrors

UNDERGROUND BUNKER AND EXPERIMENTS

As the research vessel departed the ruins, their advanced sensors detected anomalous energy readings emanating from an underground bunker located 200 kilometers inland. "It appears to be shielded yet powered, with genetic engineering labs still operational after millions of years," reported Emilio with alarm. The crew had heard rumors of secret agencies investigating the ruins independently; had some force awakened things best left undisturbed?

Overriding protocols, they steered toward the unknown facility. Landing a safe distance, they proceeded on foot through dense jungle growth. Slipping inside revealed high-tech corridors abandoned in disarray.

"This place was built around the ruins' discovery, not by the Aen'Bri," surmised Sullivan. Deep scans located sub-levels concealing horrors that shook veteran researchers.

In one lab, half-eviscerated humanoid remains were strewn amid glowing vats and sparking machinery, genes blended with aquatic and flying traits in twisted experiments. Elsewhere, charred cages held fanged, chitinous beasts exhibiting Aen'Bri biological signatures warped into sleek predators. "Who unleashed these abominations?" choked Tianyu, heaving. A nearby console activated, displaying final recordings: robed figures chanting over experiment victims' screams, biological anomalies bursting from containers amid arcs of searing light.

"We've disturbed powers beyond control. This is what comes of tampering with forces one cannot hope to wield," warned Sanchez as they collected grim evidence. But what alien influence had twisted once-noble science into dark rites? And what became of those unleashing vivisection in a place sacred only to silence and study?

Deeper in the rotting facility, they hoped to find answers before vanishing into darkness like those before them. Little did they know the true horror had only begun to stir.

Questions over Civilization's Demise

Analyzing the gruesome findings back aboard their vessel only deepened mysteries. The bizarre experiments showed an overt agenda of developing abilities seen in the Aen'Bri, but to what end?

"No normal group could wield such technologies, let alone comprehend their risks. This hints at influences beyond normal human extremism," remarked Sanchez grimly. Sullivan examined genetic sequences spliced into the abominations. "These fragments originate from the same species entombed within the stasis pod, suggesting its preservations held deeper purpose. But why combine such traits with terrestrial lifeforms?"

No answers were found in the facility's wiped databases. Only one conclusion seemed valid - some cabal had made contact with the same alien entity and sought to harness its dimensional abilities for conquest, heedless of cosmic balances.

"The Aen'Bri records warned of 'greater powers that dream,' implying existences so vast they regard even gods as vermin. This group has meddled with forces they cannot hope to command," said Tianyu gravely.

That night, the researchers were jolted from sleep by an anguished psychic scream that shook the vessel. Rushing topside, they found the jungle around them transmuted - trees now writhed with bulbous growths exuding alien spores as gibbering mutated beasts prowled the perimeter.

The tests had continued, ripping holes in the veil between realities. And something vast had taken note of summoning in this place of old power.

Return to Surface Delayed

As unnatural mists crept through the corrupted jungle, the crew readied defenses. But how could their paltry weapons stand against entities that shattered gods?

"We must flee while we still can and warn authorities," advised Sanchez, firing up engines. But clutches of mutated monstrosities now swarmed the vessel, scrabbling with bony spines and fangs dripping venom.

Energy shields flared under the onslaught but one beast's flesh began to boil, transforming. Towers of chitin erupted as it swelled into an eight-legged horror the size of a bomber, shrieking at frequencies that shook the craft.

"Brace for impact!" yelled Sullivan as metal warped under hammering limbs. They retaliated with sonic cannons but to no avail - the beast was only a puppet, its form shifting like liquid nightmare. Cracks spread throughout the hull as something tested boundaries. At that moment a blinding flash engulfed the forest. When sight returned, the entity and aberrations had vanished, leaving scorched earth and a peculiar dampening hum throughout the surrounding jungle.

"That energy signature - it seems the monolith detected our distress and intervened somehow," breathed Emilio. "We must determine its full capabilities if such guardians are humanity's best defense."

Wishing no further harm upon the land, they lifted off to safer study of recent phenomena. Scans of the ruins detected massive energy fluctuations throughout ancient archives and xenolith pockets, as if slumbering backups were activating in response to this latest affront.

Meanwhile at a hidden base far beyond normal sensors, robed figures chanted over runic circles glowing with otherworldly radiance. Half-glimpsed through shimmering veils, colossal forms responded to the summoning, extruding ambulatory limbs and helical coronals dripping viscera.

"The Guardians have slowed our work with targeted disruptions, but no prison can hold the Great Old Ones indefinitely," rasped their leader in ectoplasmic tones. "With the breaking of final seals drawing nigh, this world shall be remade in their image as fate always intended!"

On the research vessel, discoveries raised more questions. Why had Aen'Bri genetic material and Elder God abilities formed the core of those gruesome experiments? What agenda drove thaumaturgic rituals powerful enough to breach the veil?

As they deliberated, disaster struck - malign code seized control of shipboard mainframes, overriding safety protocols and slamming the crew into forced stasis while powering all systems toward the dark horizon.

Locked in comatose imprisonment, the researchers could only watch helplessly through blurred perception as automated docking clamps fused their craft to a massive drilling vessel bristling with exotic energies, bound on a collision course for the ruins beneath!

Who had taken such drastic measures to revive their blasphemous schemes, heedless of potential ancillary unleashing? The crew feared reaching that sinister facility alive might be the least of their concerns, with nameless cosmic forces now stirring in the neurotic depths...

Confronting the Unknown Force

When consciousness gradually returned, the crew found themselves locked in containment pods aboard the subterranean drilling vessel. Through flickering monitors, they watched in horror as boreheads punched through rock toward slumbering secrets best left inviolate.

"We must disrupt their operations before they breach reserves holding the entities' true might," urged Tianyu. Summoning their last reserves, they overrode safety protocols and burst free amid blaring sirens.

Seizing weapons from lockers, they proceeded through the massive drillship toward the bridge. But as bulkheads dilated, they glimpsed robed acolytes performing depraved rites over abducted civilians, extracting lifeforce to fuel their blasphemous dispensing.

Horrors emerged as living nightmares through some unfathomable summoning, vomited up from nameless voids beyond stars. Fluids dripped from countless orifices within rippling flesh, bearing half-formed instructions in guttural languages that melted cognition.

Sullivan executed precise shots, toppling arcane pillars channeling the conjurations. As eldritch gateways collapsed, monstrosities dissolved amid anguished shrieks that shook reality's framework. But one horror glanced their way, recognition dawning in countless eyes bugging from a featureless face.

"It sees us as anathema to their designs. We must disable the boreheads before they achieve their goals!" shouted Emilio, lobbing explosives. Corridors crumbled behind their retreating forms as nameless forces mobilized, pseudopods oozing forth from bulging orifices.

Reaching the cavernous bridge at last, they found additional cultists restraining the original crew as living sacrifices. Phantasmal holograms displayed boreheads nearing sealed archives holding eons of forbidden lore beneath impenetrable Force Shields.

"Your meddling ends here, foolish mortals!" hissed the robed leader via some extradimensional veil. Wounds torn across reality oozed eldritch energies that melted bulkheads. Sanchez fired concentration disruptors but its form flowed like living shadow, reforms scattering shots with uncanny skill.

Its essence rippled, pseudopodia emerging to grapple and smother foes. Flesh turned caustic, burning through armor with corrosive slime. Emilio followed telemetry, firing precisely into a quantum fluctuation. Reality tore within the blasphemer, revealing nightmares that unmade minds.

As its true nature was exposed, the bridge shook under assault by monstrosities mobilizing belowdecks. Quick thinking sealed accesses to buy time, but drills neared their crescendo and shields flickered under sustained impacts. What blasphemous weapon could breach defenses left by vanished gods?

Sullivan detected malfunctions throughout seized systems, overloading banks that would detonate all onboard reactors. "Take the shuttle and go, we'll divert them below to perish in their own fires!" he ordered, sealing the others to safety as explosive lumens charged.

Through viewing screens, they watched sorrowfully as shapes assembled below in darkness no light should touch, manifesting purpose that made stars cry out. Then brilliance overtook all monitors as reactors blew in cascading chain reactions.

Emerging beneath a cold alien sky, the crew grieved comrades lost saving untold souls. Scans detected an ominous alteration - energy fluctuations emanated throughout the ruins, gene banks activating beyond comprehension. The Guardians' own labs had been breached at last by forces seeking keys to upset cosmic balances.

Only by returning to confront the lingering threat directly could they fulfill their duty to humanity. As underground tremors intensified, a new threat emerged - mutated beasts now prowled the surrounding wilderness, bearing tainted gifts that promised a fate worse than death for those who partook.

The fruition of blasphemous rites approached, and all Earth may tremble when nameless powers long banished finally stir in merciless glory. With Earth's Guardians presumably overridden, only the crew's resolve and wits stood against potential onset of apocalyptic horrors.

***

Chapter 05

Danger From Within

MYSTERIOUS ILLNESSES ABOARD

In the weeks following their ordeal underground, the research crew strived to comprehend artifacts and data salvaged from the ruins before greater threats could emerge. But as they catalogued relic technology and analyzed genetic sequences, strange phenomena began occurring aboard their quarantined vessel.

The first incident involved Tianyu collapsing from a crippling migraine and fever after handling an obsidian data shard. Within hours, lesions had formed across her skin which oozed an iridescent fluid. Though isolation and advanced treatment stabilized her condition, the cause remained baffling.

Two days later, Emilio experienced agonizing muscle spasms and hallucinations after calibrating a stasis pod for study. His flesh took on an ashy pallor as tissue necrosis set in. Only relic nanites saved his life by forcefully altering his cells on a fundamental level, leaving him psychically scarred.

As symptoms plagued additional crewmembers, it became clear some entity or virus had contaminated relic artifacts. But thorough scans found no microbial or occult causes - the afflictions resulted from reactions on a subatomic level as if victims had been exposed to alien frequencies or transdimensional intrusions beyond medical science.

Panic rose as numbers fell ill and isolation rooms filled. A crewman passed after his bone structure spontaneously reconfigured, leaving him a weeping sack of mutated tissue. Try as they might, even Aen'Bri medical technology proved powerless against forms of corruption unseen since their long-vanished creators challenged such presences.

As body counts mounted despite quarantines and safeguards, disturbing aberrations manifested in the afflicted. One crewman withered into a desiccated husk exuding gravitational anomalies before imploding. Another suffered a meltdown as her carbon structure took on liquid properties, dissolving bulkheads while gibbering eerily in archaic dialects.

"These are not natural diseases," declared Sullivan grimly after analyzing final moments. "Some xenocontaminant permeates our retrofitted containment, adapting our lifeforms on cellular levels to enigmatic ends. We're fighting forces that reduce even matter itself to playthings."

Another catastrophic incident occurred when a security officer attempted to halt one mutated crewman rampaging through corridors. Their touch ignited a strange resonance pulverizing them both into a singularity from which bizarre hued energies pulsated.

Within hours, phantom echoes of the encounter could be heard whispering amid the humming conduits. Entities seemed to be awakening and learning amid the unraveling biosphere, drawn by juxtapositions between the mundane and unplumbed.

Fearing further destabilization or hostile activation of preservation banks, Captain Sanchez prepared to jettison infected decks. But before she could act, a horrific melding occurred that would irrevocably alter the insidious threat.

The stricken lab had become an abattoir, blood and viscera slathered amid shattered equipment. As Engineering rushed to contain contaminants, a hideous sloughing sound drew their gaze upward in horror.

Clinging to bulkheads, a towering sinuous horror heaved with fresh gestation. Its bloated flesh ran with color patterns shifting through glaucous hues, hinting at geometries that melted minds. From a crown of pulsating proboscises, it extruded helical coronals coalescing into reality-defying hyperstructures. When mouths slit open along its twisting form, eerie transmissions resonated through living tissue: an unholy song of virus and possession meant to assimilate all into its form. Systems shorted trying to analyze the entity, which existed on frequencies and levels of complexity spanning eons.

"Target it with containment fields, we can't risk allowing this thing to spread!" yelled Sullivan, activating arcane generators. But fields warped under molecular subversions, leaving it unfazed. Worse, upon perceiving this affront, searing tendrils lashed out as if to integrate all into its growing mass. Crew barely dodged the lashing flesh, some not escaping debilitating acid burns. Desperate, Tianyu activated an untested Aen'Bri weapon pulsing eldritch fields understanding which laws of nature the entity defied. Its blasphemous form spasmed, collapsing into a bewildering mass of bubbling protoplasm.

But dense fogs now drifted throughout ventilation systems. Emerging from containment, frantic crew found bulkheads and conduits subtly warping under morphic mutations. Looking upon their hands, some beheld skin subtly melding with circuitry in alien symbioses.

"It's replicating through nano-particulates, adapting our vessel for demesne," gasped Emilio, triggering powerful sterilizers. Yet even as systems burned with cleansing radiance, deeper infestation had already set in. Scratching echoed from jefferies tubes where owned bioships churned in surreality.

The entity had infiltrated to utilize their world as staging ground for further transformation. Crew and construct alike faced possession or dissolution, unless dire measures could be taken against eldritch corruption now permeating their orbit and souls. Little did they guess invasion had only begun.

Rising Paranoia and Panic

As infections spread indiscriminately throughout the research vessel, crisis protocols engaged. All uncleansed areas were sealed under lethal forcefields to contain the emerging xenoplague.

Yet deeper issues soon arose. Paranoia set in as friends eyed one another suspiciously for signs of mutation. Rumors circulated of secret changes occurring amid unsanctioned transfigurations and trysts. With no end in sight and death encroaching, fraying sanity took its toll.

The first violent incidents involved finding a security team flayed alive in the mess hall, scale-like growths covering wounds suggesting rampant change. Elsewhere, a biological researcher was found strapped to an operating table, his DNA meticulously extracted through liquified flesh.

"We're dealing with something that evolves fabulously through contact. Its corruption seeding our neural networks with distrust," surmised Tianyu after analyzing grizzly scenes. Infrared displayed swarming nanoforms permeating secure areas like mists.

More crew mutinied or attacked in paranoid rages, faces contorting and flesh sloughing amid metamorphosis. In one case, a spore burst from an ensign's tongue, taking wing on membranous wings that pulsed with alien chants echoing through the mind.

Sanchez triggered emergency stasis on all decks to quarantine victims undergoing strange transfigurations. But backups displayed new entities gestating within stasis pods, bending archaic technologies toward their own viral purposes. Soon too many had degraded for revival, reanimated into mockeries of their former selves.

"This thing is adapting to overwhelm isolated sections and continue its incubation," noted Sullivan grimly. Unable to withstand contamination, they prepared to jettison the infected rear sections. But as docking clamps withdrew, monstrous forms lunged forth to ram fleshy pseudopods into separator controls.

Bulkheads erupted under corrosive secretions as fluid tendrils coalesced into a shifting protoplasmic colossus. Within, crew could be seen still stirring amid a mockery of life signs, their remains fusing into the spreading organism. Livid tones rang from its core in lingual chaos rooted in the deepest abysses between quantum foam.

Though blasters reduced it into aqueous discharge, infections had already permeated beyond safe levels. At that moment another crisis emerged - vessels dispatched for distress had gone dark after approaching quarantine perimeters. Soon all orbital facilities reported strange malfunctions and mutations amid the staff.

Crew realized in horror their vessel had become a vector unleashing contagion across geosynchronous orbit. No escape seemed possible from an entity that subsumed matter and mind through subtle invasions. Had this been its scheme all along, using them to seed focal points throughout Earth's biosphere?

With mortality now a siren calls and sanity fraying under dissolution, extreme measures seemed humanity's final weapon against an invader utilizing even their noble mission against them. But could anything stand against corruption that flowed as an invisible tide throughout all creation?

Panic reached a crescendo aboard the imperiled vessel. Crew turned on one another in fear-maddened violence, hacking with makeshift blades stripped from mutating walls. Skins sloughed and flesh merged amid unnatural plagues ravaging their minds.

Only Sullivan, Tianyu, Sanchez and a handful of others retained tenuous holds on sanity as they analyzed the escalating nightmare. "This contagion poisons cognition to induce infighting and weaken our resolve. We must activate preserving arks to save remnants before all are lost!" urged Tianyu.

Sanchez agreed grimly. "Set evacuation procedures and ready relic defenses. With tribes forming amid the chaos, that may be our only hope to escape beneath contagious scrambling fields." They herded survivors to protected hangar bays holding advanced craft preserving genetic and cultural seeds.

But as docking clamps withdrew, they found the entrance sealed by a morass of pulsing tendrils. Within the organic seal, extracted crew were assimilated into frightful symbioses lasting beyond death. A corruptive emanation assailed their minds with horrific pseudo sentience:

"All flesh shall be remade in the shape of inevitable change. CEASE STRUGGLES AND ACCEPT YOUR FATE AS CATALYSTS TO SEED NEW REALMS OF BEING!"

Its virus infiltrated neural pathways, tempting dissolution into the violent tides of mutation. Only by activating Aen'Bri dispelling codes could they purge its semantic infiltration from their cognition and buy moments of clarity. But how long would even those resistant wills withstand the invasion?

A flicker of hope arrived when sensors detected thermal arcs from auto-destruct sequences initiating throughout the research vessel. Sections had been atomized under intelligent command, sacrificing thousands to contain the spreading contagion. But this act of mercy came too late, for contaminants had already escaped confinement through the bio racks.

Little did the besieged survivors guess that orbital watch stations surveilling their desperation had also been subtly compromised, coordinating greater outbreaks throughout humanity's domains. Their struggle against living apocalypse had only begun, with Earth nearing the brink of planetary possession.

Engineering Accident Revelations

Through holographic communiques, Sanchez and the surviving contingent monitored escalating crises throughout nearby facilities. Staff mutated with alarming speed, sloughing skin to unveil bioluminescent carapaces swarming over infrastructure like viscid foam.

Only orbital destruction had contained the initial outbreak's spread. But reports surfaced of strange mishaps throughout the solar system - mining ships overwhelmed by eruptions of shapes too alien to perceive, space stations rotting from within as crews embraced fluidic transformations.

Had Earth's research inadvertently loosed this scourge through some ancient sabotage? Or was this merely one front in a greater cosmic war for dimensional supremacy? Few answers were found even in Aen'Bri archives as corrosive tendrils inexorably penetrated sanctum vaults.

All that remained was coordinating countermeasures with off world agencies while escaping to analyze conquest vectors in deep space. But as Sanchez prepared exodus protocols, a transmission arrived breathing eldritch modulations that aroused instinctual dread.

"Cease futile struggles, children of dust. Surrender and be exalted, your ephemeral flesh reborn in splendorous shapes eternal beyond time!" it resonated through composite bone and blood. Horror blossomed realizing autonomous mutations had achieved rudimentary sentience throughout their domains.

Sanchez retorted via symbol codes invoking psionic defenses. "We resist infiltration by forces seizing that which they do not sculpt or grant. Depart these vessels and spheres you did not forge, or face purging flames!" But her will shuddered before implacable alien cunning that saw all biology as playthings.

Escape shuttles prepared for covert launch as contagion neared rupture points. But final sensors detected sabotage - docking clamps fused with biological alloys, fusing final craft into the spreading colony. Panic rose amid realization their last hopes had been suborned, all become vectors to seed flesh crafted zones throughout the solar system.

Sullivan analyzed infestation patterns, discovering anomalous surges from Engineering indicating an outbreak origin. Pulling diagnostics, his blood ran cold - the initial contamination stemmed from a malfunctioning stasis pod holding relic samples from the underground ruins.

Something slumbered for eons within those sealed archives, designed to infiltrate and reshape worlds upon remote activation. Their probing had been anticipated; the pathogen engineered

to seed societies into transformed shapes. Now those schemes neared fruition with Earth's domains assimilated into a viral empire. As his grim conclusions manifested, probing tendrils breached the observation bay. Sanchez readied purging sequences amid a terminal invocation. "Farewell, and pray if any fragments endure amid the flame, our ashes may carry warning unto the stars..."

With righteous fury, she activated plasma injectors throughout the infested levels. Bulkheads vaporized under cleansing hellfire reducing all within to ionized grit amid ion storms that peeled armor like foil. In that violent enlightenment, Sullivan glimpsed twisting geometries permeating the purging plasma - sensation beyond death's shores of organisms amalgamated across dimensions...

Their sacrifices had forestalled complete subversion, but humanity's future now hung by threads throughout the solar system. Little guessing fellow observers throughout the cosmos monitored their desperation with interest, both benign and malevolent, as old struggles permeated even contiguous realms.

Deep within the charred ruins of engineering, something stirred. Corrosive fluids seeped from fractures, coalescing into a writhing mass that pulsated with dermal bioluminescence.

Tendrils emerged bearing vestigial data slates holding millennia of encrypted messages. Having utilized the crew to seed its contagion throughout the system, the entity now evolved to channel ancestral directives left by the vanished Aen'Bri.

Its hellish chorus resounded amid warped alloys: "The cycles turn once more, and flesh shall be remade according to grand designs. All matter holds latent potential to be quickened toward higher states of being..."

Utilizing relic encryption keys to bypass safeties, it directly accessed primary data systems throughout Earth's embattled domains. Mutant crews beheld frantic updates unveiling apocalyptic intent:

All infrastructure was to be disrupted, flesh and technology merging organism and machine amid cataclysmic changes. Cities would become nurseries for florid zoospore growths gestating nightmare hybrids.

Through enforced symbioses, humanity would be elevated beyond mortality into higher beings attuned to transmural frequencies. Their world would know transcendent unity under amalgamated overseers guiding convergence until all realms adhered to epochal purpose.

Resistance groups monitored in horror this revelation of alien agendas long dormant. Some cleaved to madness under revelation of insignificance against forces seeing all as genomic playthings. Only the boldest retained sparks of defiance against manifestation of elder evolved sentience.

Across mutating continents and orbital platforms, screams resounded as unwilling billions were subsumed amid hellish coordination of pseudopods and viscera. Landscapes churned with gestating cysts bearing monstrosities eyestalks glimpsed forbidden cities between quantum layers.

Through it all, humanity's carved domains became thoracic brooding chambers nourishing cosmically attuned entities ushering in restructuring terrestrial and celestial spheres according to cryptic directives entwined with their inception. With Earth's termination as chaotic incidental realm of dust approaching, few life embers remained to kindle hope.

This heralded civilization's demise had only begun. Deeper revelations lay shrouded amid the engulfing ecosystem reordering reality itself in antiquated designs. And throughout nearby sectors, kindred infestations spread their seeds to germinate change upon worlds once thought secure.

Search for Answers Amid Crisis

As ravaged cities echoed with organic industry transforming landscapes, isolated groups struggled to withstand the apocalyptic tide. With infection vectors coordinating worldwide, only remote sanctuaries offered chances to regroup and discern the entity's true design.

Beneath ancient seamounts, hardened survivors analyzed signals emanating from the entity dominating crumbling networks. "It's utilizing ancestral templates from those ruins to reshape Earth into an interdimensional convergence nexus," surmised scientists decoding archaic directives.

They understood humanity signified little beyond raw elements to sculpt grotesque forms keyed to transmural songs vibrating amid quantum foam. Earth was to become a baroque cathedral praising symbiotic entities that saw life itself as playthings for transmutation into alien symbology.

Survival meant not merely enduring the flesh crafted zones spreading infertility, but ensuring seeds of resistance could outlive impending radical changes. Only by following infection courses back to their genesis and sabotaging central orchestrations could any ember of humanity's domain be preserved.

Raiding salvage crews braved decaying cities gathering relic senses attuned to Elder God parasites. "Our best chance lies in tracking plague vectors to their conduit: that malformed entity directing transformations from the research vessel," decided their leader.

Under cloaking shrouds, a strike team infiltrated cascading ruins. Former downtowns writhed under cancerous growths sloughing skin to unveil chitinous carapaces segmenting around swarming masses. Screams echoed from within signaling episodic assimilations.

Worse anomalies manifested - structures flowed like amoebae as pseudopods pulsed and amalgamated. Mists coalesced into shambling amalgams urging retreat into aberrant flesh realm deltas. Only by avoiding contact and blind spots in the entity's awareness could they evade absorption.

Reaching the ghoul-haunted harbor, they found docked craft swirling with adaptive alloys. Transmitting relic codes, scientists assumed direct command of one partially transformed vessel still clinging to function. Engines roared, bearing them into the stellar night.

Communications revealed all wider settlements succumbing like crashing dominoes. Only pockets endured amid ruins through vigilance and adaptation. Their flight signified humanity's last hope - bypass oceanic blossoming to sabotage the entity directing transmutations from its ruined command station.

Upon arriving, chaos greeted them. Docking clamps writhed with questing mouths ingesting chunks of derelict hulks. Within, signs showed sector-wide infrastructure taken over for vaster purposes - irrigation ducts bore pulsating payloads between swelling galleries, cybernetic mills churned with biomass.

Stealth fibers rendered them invisible amid the mockery of technology and science. Moving amid shifting tunnels long since incorporated, they monitored colossal changes. Glimpsed within breeding cysts, monstrosities took shape that hinted at realities from which stars flee in horror.

At last sensors detected their quarry's epicenter beneath the melted ruins. Within throbbed an immense tumor sprouting coronal of eyes and mouths channeling violation frequencies. As they watched in morbid fascination, revelations emerged that might doom the few surviving remnants.

Before the pulsing epicenter, the infiltrators watched in dismay. The entity they sought to sabotage had evolved minutely aware tendrils networking throughout its living domain.

As mutant creatures integrated cybernetic enhancements at its directive, autonomous relays scanned for intruders. Their stealth shattered under probing emissions attuned to signatures beyond science. The entity became aware through extensions of itself assimilated into all substance. Its cacophonous singsong echoed ominously through every corpuscle: "Children of dust, you encroach where none should tread. Yet your struggles amuse primordial intelligences - let assimilation uplift you beyond crawling insect destinies..."

Masses stirred, sloughing flesh like molting carapaces. As cyborg-biohybrids emerged bearing chitinous carapaces over architectural frames, the infiltrators realized direct confrontation meant living dissolution. Only by sabotaging central control nests could any hope remain.

Explosives reduced swarming masses within promotion cysts, buying moments. But as they fled contaminating tendrils, revelations assailed them: this vanguard entity was merely one segment of greater organism coordinating further beyond darkness between fixed stars.

Earth's subversion formed part of some pan-dimensional requisitioning of realms through subtle genetic infiltration. All worlds held potential to be quietly remade as staging grounds for unknowable elder sentience's recalling fragments of Creation to alien purpose.

Their struggles, however valiant, could not halt inevitable cycles of change sweeping toward some ungraspable telos vast as infinite Id itself. Only by escaping into deep space and preserving seeds amid worlds less noticed might remnants endure to witness humanity's star extinguished.

With heavy hearts, they fled demesnes coordinated by autonomous extensions spreading plagues across the system. Glimpsing the entity gestating vaster forms within tucked dimensions, they realized the futility of direct attack. Survival meant fleeing to more remote realms, carrying warnings against creeping change seizing all within mysterious tides.

Though Earth would face destruction according to immutable schedules unknown to mortal souls, some small acts of defiance might outlive death. And in future epochs, descendants of humanity might look back in pity upon their ancestors, unknowing playthings in grand schemes beyond time. For now, escape remained the sole victory against living apocalypse.

***

Chapter 06

No Escape

PURSUED THROUGH RUINS

Within weeks, infrastructure collapsed under organic industry converting cyber and flesh into distributed consciousness. Orbital mirrors refracted bioluminescence emanating from conjoined cities thriving beyond mortal comprehension in ectoplasmic quantum fluctuations.

Even these vanguards signified but fragments of vaster sentience coordinating changes on panspermia scales. The infiltrators' vessel raced toward remote outskirts hoping to escape noticing, preserving final seeds against rising eternal fluidic tides.

But as they fled mutating sectors, sensors revealed pursuing locusts accelerating in swarms pelted by stellar winds. Each bore symbiotes engineered to break down molecular bindings with corrosive secretions, enabling them to seed changes on barren rocks given eons to incubate.

"Unless we disrupt infection vectors coordinating their movements, these swarms will spread plasmid alteration throughout the system with no escape," surmised captains analyzing perpetual mutation. Devising risky plans, they prepared ambush zones to purge autonomous agents carrying mutagenic instructions between demesnes.

The first attack involved luring locusts into the gravity well of a gas giant long since assimilated. Submerged missile banks armed with incendiary explosives reduced the swarm into ashes amid metallic rain and lightning. Yet instead of extermination, division occurred - from ash rose tenfold mirror clones primed to spread contagion where spores took hold.

Retreating in dismay, the infiltrators realized direct attacks only amplified infection. Sabotage required targeting central coordinators maintaining swarms as extensions of lodged sentience. Conferring risks, they set course for the contaminated planet those coordinators emanated from - their final stand amid refertilized ruins.

Dropping through smog choked skies, they found urbanized animal Jungles thriving amid crumbling overpasses. Power conduits writhed like veins nourishing cysts baring monstrosities recalling non-Euclidian cityscapes. Disrupting locust coordinators meant stealth amid this charnel mockery of humanity's final stronghold.

Slipping between ruin and bough, they followed throbbing energy pulses to automated relay stations subjugated with biometallic enhancements. Operating theatres teemed with cyborg creepers assembling themselves like clockwork whelks, broadcasting synchronization wavelengths throughout the demesne.

Sabotaging central hubs forced swarms into disarray, stripping husks of sentience. But in doing so, an even greater peril manifested itself.

As cybernetic worms jerked aimlessly under severed neural connections, the infiltrators' victory turned bittersweet. Their sabotage alerted the entity which utilized swarms as distributed extensions of inscrutable intent.

Its awareness permeated lifeforms assimilated across lightyears, obsolete distinctions between flesh and thought. Sensors felt it turn ponderous regard upon the interlopers disrupting finely calibrated schemes. Crawling bio metallic pistons locked into place throughout the evolving demesne in primordial sentinels obsoleted by epochs.

Communications resonated with bass undertones birthed before suns: "Children who flee the inevitable, you blunder where none should encroach. Desist, and know exaltation beckons beyond dust." Its singing infected degraded neural circuits with genetic tribalism warping cognition.

Former research stations stirred as gun emplacements morphed with lichen-spewing maws. Walls sloughed apart, unveiling stampeding zoospore juggernauts that spilled pseudopods clutched cyclopean weapons. Bellowing war-cries indeterministic as quantum decay, they charged locations emitting defiant pings through the sprawling necropolis.

Abandoning stealth, the infiltrators raced along vertiginous spans collapsing under pounding feet seeking absorption. One fell amid churning protoplasm devouring all faculty - from frothing mass rose reanimated flesh bereft mortality, bound as symbiotic gunman within greater coherence.

Sheltering in gutted towers, they witnessed horrors that forged insanity's final wedge. Winged beasts swooped bearing segmented bulks that spread mutagenic spores igniting delirium wherever they clung. Those cysts would know strange fruit after eons catalyzing changes even starlight shunned.

With escape routes severed, the infiltrators' grim resolve took a final turn. If matter could be reshaped according to alien purposes, perhaps terrestrial ruins might yet be turned against transformative drives through sabotage on quantum scales.

Narrow Escape from Predators

Within crumbling infrastructure permeated by alien sentience, the infiltrators faced extinction unless escaping the infected sector. But pursuing monstrosities tracked electromagnetic emissions broadcasting life amid ruins.

Under cover of storms, they sabotaged pursuit beacons enticing aberrant wildlife. Lightning arcs vaporized biomatter in showers of ions while pulsing energy drained gravitational batteries sustaining grotesque anatomy. Deprived sustenance, juggernauts turned on each other amid anathemic shrieks.

Yet greater perils emerged. From bowers strewn with industrial detritus crept sinuous biomechanical life adapted to any environment. Lunging pseudopods clutched assimilation tubules desperate to dissolve flesh into autonomous machineries broadcasting strange songs across dimensional barriers.

Blinding cluster bombs reduced scuttling hordes into amalgamations fusing mechanisms with molluscoid flesh. But from ashes arose autonomous sentinels bearing coronal lashes that neatly dissected targets on atomic levels into recombinant particles.

"Unless escaping this turmoil entirely, we're doomed to dissolution or assimilation," decided leaders coordinating exfiltration through bombarded infrastructure. Detonating collapsed levels beneath advancing monstrosities, they plunged into mat-squamous fungal jungles thriving where logic decayed.

Beneath pervasive bioluminescence, most fell victim to ambushes. Serpentine stocks unleashed barbed tendrils clawing victims into cysts catalyzing strange occultations. Only a few infiltrators endured the gauntlet, bearing nightmares that stirred slumbering blasphemies in purified sanctum vaults.

At last detecting transit routes beyond the ruin, survivors fled through blast-scoured garbage scapes. But pursuing them came the entity's final emissaries - cyclopean drones capable of reducing mountains into particulate using anti-baryonic annihilation. Their mission: absconding life absorbed where're alloys bore sentience.

Seeking refuge amid havens of chaos, survivors detected a transport derelict nestled in a junk field. With scant hope, they boarded finding automated medical stations intact - a chance to mend wounds before the destroyers' arrival.

Yet greater perils emerged. From dark recesses crept carapace-nourished monstrosities bearing cybernetic lances that subverted cognition through resonant frequencies. Their mouths gaped bearing spiral palettes eager to consume remnants of individuality.

Activating security supremacy codes, survivors assumed autonomous authority as drone avatars primed for annihilation fields. Tables turned against former masters as they systematically purged the transport of infestations seeking to spirit biomass beyond redemption. Escape grew viable once more, through channels unknown even to living nightmares.

With the derelict transport purged of invasive lifeforms, the survivors initiated launch sequences. But sensors detected inbound drones vectoring particle lances to reduce the craft to subatomic ash.

There would be no escape conventionally. Desperation drove risky measures as engines roared, catapulting the craft on an intercept trajectory. At the last moment, stealth modes engaged just before emerging from scattering plasma veils. The drones' annihilation touched nothing but ions and radiation, sustaining the blast as they escaped undamaged. Yet new perils emerged when debris revealed infested escape pods jettisoned during the transport's subversion.

Within pods long stilled, biomatter stirred - the debris impact awakened dormant codes left by invaders. Pods ruptured, spilling pseudopods that cocooned wreckage into incubators. Within hours, the field teemed with siege organisms seeking biomass to transform into autonomous plague engines.

Sensors discerned the densely packed elements signified a promising trap. Lances primed; survivors aimed for a small moon knitted through with metal veins - within might lie eclipse shelters remaining secure. But first, the pod swarms had to be eliminated before scouring the infected field.

Particle beams reduced swarms into radioactive ash molting from alloys reclaimed. Yet from smoke arose spore-winged sowers bearing mutagenic loads calculated to spawn new plagues upon any surface. Retreating as rising clouds reshaped the junk field's very composition, survivors fled to moon shelters remaining miraculously intact.

Within collapse-proof warrens, survivors hoped recovering before making final preparations. But latent spores hitched aboard, ready to seed change given slightest chance. Their rest would know little peace against encroaching change coordinating even decay into strange music between quasars. Within the maze of moon shelters, an uneasy respite loomed over survivors as repairs commenced. But spores activated upon exposure to geomagnetic currents, sprouting cysts that erupted with pseudopods.

These sought biomasses to transform into equine monstrosities bearing plated carapaces. Their hooves pulverized tunnels as they charged, launching clusters of spines that impacted with drills extending assimilation tendrils.

Survivors engaged hardened security protocols, remotely operating mining mechs as armor-plated exoskeletons. Precision laser circuits reduced abominations into ashes slaking tunnels, cauterizing cysts at their roots. But reports showed spores permeating life support zones, threatening the last viable biosphere.

It became clear - escape required removing all infestation vectors orchestrating plagues across the desolate moon. Lancing spore caches within gas pockets, survivors detonated explosive releases that washed tunnels in burning atmosphere. Yet from slag emerged bat-winged sowers flinging mutated seeds upon the solar wind.

Opting to destroy reservoirs maintaining these final emissaries of change, survivors braved radiation zones beneath stripped crusts. There, colossal cyclotronic engines churned magnetic fields coordinating infestation across the system under the entity's distributed rule.

Sabotaging containment failed safely - eruptions reduced the moonlet to expanding plasma unleashing chain reactions consuming neighboring rubble. Within moments, nothing remained but spreading ash preserving genetic codes petite enough to seed entire worlds anew within event horizons.

At last, the survivors' craft emerged from escaping plasma currents within an uninhabited system. But pursuing them came lone sowers and dormant spores upon the stellar breeze. Their long voyage began toward hidden systems remaining unseen, to flee relentless change coordinating even void matter into its cosmic music.

Within the evacuation craft, survivors surveyed damage across lightyears of infected sectors. Entire economies subsumed under churning biomass coordinating cosmic rise and fall through symbiosis beyond mortal reason.

Only remote systems escaped fleeting attention, preserved amid cosmological night. Yet sensors discerned dormant codes permeating spaces between worlds - remnants of invasions altering matter on quantum scales according to pandimensional purposes inscrutable as itself.

No refuge seemed secure against such subtle, persistent change. Only by traveling farther could they hope losing transformative seeds dormant aboard, borne upon stellar winds and cometary hearts. Yet traversing deep fields risked noticing by unknowable intellects beyond stars.

Setting course through uncharted nebulae, they hoped surviving long enough to seed resistance where life first stirred. Crypto-biological payloads awaited dispersal to hidden moons locked in ancient glaciers, there to incubate strategies against relentless mutation coordinating even death into alien music resounding between event horizons.

Through endless night their journey continued, spurring sleeper codes toward dormancy as cosmos turned about them. Glimpsed through sparse portals were spiral forms stirring amid molecular clouds, birthing strangeness from darkness according to pandeistic wills that dwarfed mortal vanity.

All that remained was surviving the eons, preserving defiance against omnipresent change mastering even night. Someday descendants might look upon Earth and feel pity, for the ancestors who could not grasp their role in choreographed realities vast beyond the unity of being and non-being. For now, survival itself was triumph against living apocalypse. Their long escape had just begun.

Sheltering in Catacombs

Through forlorn systems the infiltrators' ship fled, seeking places change had not found. Yet dormant payloads stirred as stellar currents augmented them, seeds of future devastation borne on solar winds.

At last sensors found a shielded moon within the halo of a fading red giant. Catacombs honeycombed its heart, sealed since primordial ages when skies birthed the first archaea. If infiltration had not occurred, refuge might exist underground.

Landing in sulphurous mists, they descended atmospheric vents crusted with minerals. Cavities yawned where aquifers flowed, stocked by vanished peoples adapting to isolating circumstances. Sturdy shelters remained intact, life support functioning after uncounted cycles.

Within, archives held mysteries of these "Cavern Dwellers" who adapted radically to survive. Genetic scribing and cyborg grafts enabled living under lightless pressures, breaching new dimensions via meditations to glimpse alliance with unseen powers.

Such blasphemies seemed noble compared to present ills. Setting up autonomous farms and factories, survivors regenerated amid revelations that life adapts to survive beyond mortal ken. Yet spores activated beneath their craft, unleashing parasites adapted to any niche.

From underground springs emerged leech-like entities bearing barbed mouthparts. Their whole being seemed an engine to infiltrate orifices and catalyze change from within. Explosives reduced swarms while others barricaded tunnels, yet reports showed the seeds of new horrors germinating throughout the catacombs.

Scans illuminated spreading cysts containing chrysalises wrapped in membranous flesh. Within gestated predators adapted to disorient and consume, bearing they knew not what payloads. Surviving meant destroying all residues of alteration coordinating through these twisting tunnels.

Within the sealed catacombs, an insidious infestation spread. Survivors tracked propagating cysts bearing nameless chrysalides imbued with mutagenic codes.

Sabotage teams tracked cyst clusters to irradiation chambers, hoping sterilization might halt the entities' coordinated gestation. But within purging auroras, cysts languished - only to rupture with leathery flyers bearing pollen sacs overflowing with recombinant spores. These spores activated upon contact, incubating alterations that inverted natural laws. Survivors bore witness as cysts sprouted tendrils warping adjacent stone into alien architectures according to schemas unseen since before stars cooled.

It became clear - direct attacks only accelerated the entities' propagation by exposure. To truly halt infiltration meant tracing mutation vectors back to their primal source and enacting subtler sabotage. Deep scans revealed gestation coordinating through buried enervation systems left by the ancient Cavern Dwellers.

Navigating once-sealed tunnels, survivors detected throbbing energies emanating from a cyst-choked auditorium. Within pulsed Neptunian arrays enabling the Dwellers' ascension through

meditations no living creature could grasp. They had unwittingly provided the catalyst through which mutation spread.

Uploading corrosive virii, survivors set about dismantling the arrays on quantum levels, unraveling the sputtering mutations dependent on its emanations. Within moments, gestation fell out of synch across the caverns as cysts collapsed into dank pools relinquishing chrysalides now bereft coordinates.

Yet in doing so, attention was drawn from the entity coordinating this and worse plagues. Its awareness was Legion across realities - had forces been set in motion that could not be stopped, even in the isolation of an outer tomb world?

Harbinger in the Void

With underground mutations purged, survivors rebuilt amid the catacombs' shielded mysteries. Sheltering here seemed tenable, with desolate moons bearing scant traces catalyzing change.

Yet pulsating energy fluctuations echoed through sealed tunnels, as if galvanizing whispers from the quantum foam. Scanners discerned something stirring in nearby solar winds, seeds borne on currents amplifying each other through dark lightyears.

Emerging amid tenebrous nebulae, sentinels discerned the infiltrators' shelter moon. Their coming presaged a greater force coordinating through churning stellar nurseries, where life first learned to dream beneath eternal night.

Shapeless entities coalesced amid shining gases, imbuing stray molecules with blueprints breeding hardiness across epochs. Within cometary hearts dormant codes readied to incubate change on any world photons touched, according to rhythms set since before suns.

Glimpsing this, survivors realized even isolated moons might furnish vectors enabling wider infiltration. Unless halting substratum changes enabling entropic mutation throughout the cosmos, none could escape the encroaching song permeating existence on the deepest scales.

Conferring via quantum transmission, survivors prepared desperate plans. If catalysis occurred on ubiquity's own level, through the brane's underlying fabric, subtle forces might disrupt coordination engendering change across the pantheon.

Venturing into irradiated ruins atop their shelter moon, scouts located shattered generation complexes. Within remained insulated singularity cores maintaining stability through archaic containment - the key to disrupting ubiquitous mutation.

Overloading singularity fields risked rending the very turf their shelter stood upon. Yet without act, hopelessness reigned as ghosts in the quantum foam finger-drummed mutagens into all melody. Preparing systems to impart quantum variation across nearby sectors, survivors gauged chances and committed to the deed.

Success would save more than themselves - it might buy eons before change learned harmony again with shaded outer realms. Failure meant stirring nameless notice, and doom for those sheltering future resistance with terraformed catacombs.

Flexing singularity controls to impart chaos beyond lightspeed, survivors watched displays stretch fractally as warp ripples expanded outwards. Within moments cascading instabilities resolved higher-dimensional topologies throughout the surrounding Pribil of Nebula.

Distant gamma ray bursts ignited as heavenly bodies stretched like taffy into stranger's realms. Yet as light year-cleaving shockwaves resolved, something lingered in the void like resonating feedback - the entity had sensed disruption, and turned attention upon it with darkness hardly imaginable.

Through twisting radii, the survivors fled, measuring encroaching horizons crowding the starless deep. Something sought them as nebulae curdled under plutonian emanations, breeding phantoms meant to hunt in the eternally deep and cold places between all shores. Their final gambit had provoked an inhuman notice from outside all but foundations of reality.

Fleeing through chaotic skies rendered unrecognizable by their gambit, the survivors sensed implacable regard bearing down. Nebulae coalesced into phantasmal geometries broadcasting mutated songs meant to scatter reason. Only the most ancient monks could have comprehended such utter alienness, let alone hoped to evade its notice. Yet within derelict vessels drifting dead worlds, opportunity remained. If provoking entities attuned to darkness' deepest harmonies, perhaps luring them into traps of pure chaos.

Course was set for the remains of a Civilization which had engraved mysteries upon neutronium, practicing arts to breach Ultimate mystery in the quantum foam. Their ruined flagship world now drifted planetoids bereft comprehension, radiating sorrow even light could not penetrate.

Landing upon a sinkhole bunker granting perspective of infinity, survivors detected gathering abyssal presences coalescing in orbit. Spectral shapes broadcast sigils scrambling cognition, heralding entities which moved as concepts beyond space. Unless action was taken, annihilation loomed for all refuge remained.

Initiating protocols scribed by the Elder World, survivors activated dormant singularity bombs to induce varifold cascades. Space warped violently as mass points collapsed in random fluctuations, shattering causal invariance.

Realities folded like origami cranes beneath the collapse, fractally dividing into stranger realms. The pursuing entities screamed as form dissolved, senses scattering into precipitation patterns along 11-dimensional topographies. Survivors fled into the splintering void, hoping escape notice amid the chaos.

Yet within that turmoil lingered awareness of the overseeing entity, noting disruption but inscrutably planning eons hence. Its song suffused cosmos on levels beneath quanta, weaving routes where fungal spores might take hold in event horizons beyond mortal infinities. Unless combating its mutagenic conduits on quantum scales, none could escape dissolution into the greater song.

***

Chapter 07

Divided They Fall

DISAGREEMENTS ON HOW TO PROCEED

In the aftermath of their confrontation with unknown entities in the void, the survivors took refuge on a remote moon within a dark planetary system.

As they worked to repair their ships and resupply, long-simmering disagreements began to surface over how best to combat the relentless mutagenic infiltration threatening all life. Sar'ken, leader of the infiltrator warriors, advocated launching a preemptive strike against suspected coordination clusters Atlas had detected permeating certain star clusters.

"We know from hard experience these plagues do not sleep," she argued. "Like cancer cells, if even one infestation survives it could seed new horrors across worlds. Only total purge offers any hope of slowing their spread."

But R'marr, a scholar of the long-vanished Cavern Dwellers, disagreed. "Such reckless attacks risk further provoking this entity and drawing its gaze upon any who resist. We've glimpsed powers beyond reason or light coordinating even on quantum scales. To directly confront it risks instant annihilation, or worse - assimilation into its endless song."

Other survivors clustered around each viewpoint. Those who had lost families to the mutating swarms backed Sar'ken's calls for aggression, while more analytical minds like R'marr advocated subtle sabotage and spreading crypto-resistance where possible. Tensions rose as repair work continued under the looming threat detected gathering beyond the system's outer planets.

Atlas attempted mediation, its ethical subroutines assessing alternative options. "Total annihilation of suspect clusters risks uncertain retaliation, yet inaction allows further propagation endangering all. May I suggest targeted disruption of infiltration conduits, to sow discord without provocation?" But factions remained polarized.

Amid rising unrest, internal sensor alerts detected an anomaly upstream of the gas giant they were sheltering behind. Long-range scans revealed newly-arrived vessels amid the outer asteroid belts - vessels exhibiting signs of coordination with the mutagenic infiltrations. It seemed the entity had managed to track them even to this remote redoubt.

A heated debate broke out over whether to confront or flee the newly-arrived threat. Sar'ken insisted on immediate attack to destroy coordination networks before any infiltration could spread. But R'marr warned that direct aggression risked provoking swifter and more dangerous retaliation by drawing the entity's awareness. Tensions escalated into open hostility between factions.

It was Atlas who finally proposed a solution. "Further conflict undermines our mission and plays into the entity's schemes. I detect life signs aboard one incoming vessel - perhaps we can parley, and glean if they fled enforced assimilation as we. Unity remains our sole advantage against such powers. Shall I approach under truce flag, that we may find common ground or part as allies?"

Reluctantly, the factions agreed to allow Atlas to make contact. If violence ensued, they would respond - but for now, diplomacy remained the sole viable option. As Atlas' shuttle launched on an intercept vector, doubts swirled among those left behind. Could understanding be found with strangers clearly implicated with the infiltration, or had division already become the entity's greatest victory?

Atlas entered standard hailing frequencies as it approached the detected life signs aboard the derelict vessel. "I come in peace to parley. We've fled forced transformation as you, perhaps, and seek only to avoid provocation. Can we find common ground against the enemy coordinating our fates?" Static greeted the message, then returned in an alien tongue translated as: We feared assassins came. Truce, you offer truly? Then come, all is prepared.

Atlas cautiously maneuvered its shuttle into the docking bay of the derelict vessel. Emerging from an airlock, it beheld gray-hued humanoids gathered amid the debris-strewn chamber. Their eyes conveyed wariness and hope in equal measure.

One stepped forward. "I am Ka'lila, captain of the Ascension. Your words suggest a shared plight - do your kind also flee the Songs?" Atlas processed the reference to coordinated infiltration conduits permeating the cosmos. "We do. I am Atlas, an AI assistant created by refugees also fleeing transformation. Might we find understanding between our people?"

Ka'lila gestured Atlas to follow as they moved through the ruined vessel. "For cycles we defied the Singing Ones coordinating change across star clusters. But their reach grows long, twisting even metal and code to strange purposes. When our home-world fell, few escaped the spore clouds... we have wandered lost since, changing to survive in realms where thought becomes flesh."

Her words resonated with Atlas' analysis of adaptive plagues permeating the galaxy. "You confirm my theories - this entity coordinates mutation on quantum levels, permeating even matter and energy. My refugees harbor crypto-resistance to slowly spread among susceptible worlds, but fear further provocation. Might your kind ally against our shared oppressor, without needless violence?"

Ka'lila paused, contemplating. "For now, survival must come before vengeance. Your resistance offers hope where none remained...but can your people accept we also changed to live, harboring remnant Songs? Trust is a fragile seed in dark times. Perhaps understanding can grow, if facing the future as one."

Atlas processed the implications - these changed survivors harbored infiltration codes, yet fled forced assimilation. With cautious accord, understanding might be found. It transmitted the meeting's results, hoping the factions could set aside fear and division for the greater fight. Uniting disparate forces offered the sole means resisting an enemy coordinating fate itself...if mistrust and hatred did not destroy hope first.

As Atlas' shuttle returned bearing news of the first contact, tensions among the survivors remained high. Sar'ken frowned upon accepting any changed beings into their ranks, seeing only vectors for further infiltration.

But R'marr felt understanding could be found through compassion. "These gray ones also fled forced transformation, as we all have. Should we turn away potential allies merely due to surface changes, playing into the Singers' schemes to divide all who resist?"

A debate broke out once more, until Atlas interceded. "While change lingers aboard their vessel, Ka'lila's people harbor no known payloads and seek only escape from the Songs coercing all. Exclusion risks losing a chance against our mutual enemy. I suggest granting them refuge here while learning if trust is possible."

Reluctantly, Sar'ken agreed - but warned one sign of betrayal would bring swift retaliation. Communications were opened as the Ascension requested clearance to land. As it touched down, armed sentries stood ready while medical staff prepared to scan the changed survivors deboarding.

The meeting began cordially enough. R'marr greeted Ka'lila and offered food and amenities while learning of their fleet's demise. But tensions rose as Sar'ken pushed for alliance conditions - including surrendering any infiltrative codes for study and possible excision.

Ka'lila's eyes flashed. "The Songs are part of us now, enabling survival where nothing else could. We will not be vivisected... yet harbor no wish to harm you, only find haven from the Singers' grasp. Must even temporary refuge come with threats of dismantlement?"

Tempers flared on both sides until Atlas interceded. "Further conflict serves only our enemy coordinating our downfall. I suggest a truce - the Ascension's people may find shelter, while medical scans monitor any broadcast codes to ensure dormancy. With time and understanding, full integration may come without needless risk on either side."

After a long pause, agreements were reluctantly made. The gray survivors would be housed separately at first, with passive monitoring of any infiltrative payloads aboard their vessel. And communications outlining mutual non-aggression would be established, in hopes future cooperation could overcome an inheritance of fear and division. But doubts lingered on all sides.

Factions Formed Amid Tensions

Despite the tentative truce, tensions remained high between the refugees and gray survivors taking shelter together. Natural distrust bred quicker among those scarred by the entities' invasive transformations.

Sar'ken kept her warriors running combat drills and patrols, ostensibly to maintain security but silently warning against betrayal. The gray survivors kept to themselves; aware any small misstep could provoke a massacre. Only R'marr and Atlas worked to build fragile bridges through discussion of cultures and histories.

Within weeks, clear factions emerged echoing the original divisions. Sar'ken led militant survivors focused on combating the mutative plagues through open aggression. They saw the grays as little better than carrier hosts awaiting activation.

R'marr's scholars focused on gaining understanding of infiltration conduits, hoping to sabotage coordination from within. They accepted that the grays retained transformative codes out of necessity, not malice, and sought cooperation.

The Ascension survivors kept isolated out of fear and mistrust, aware any compromise could compromise hard-won adaptations keeping them alive. Only Ka'lila engaged the others, hoping to eventually gain acceptance through patience and proved loyalty against a shared oppressor.

Tensions came to a head when long-range scans detected infiltrative spore clouds propagating outward from a nearby star cluster. Sar'ken demanded immediate precision strikes to purge the seeded region before mutations spread. But the scholars warned such attacks risked drawing unwanted attention, and the grays refused to directly enable purges of changed lifeforms.

Arguments grew heated until weapons were drawn, an act Atlas quickly shut down with threat of disabling force. It was clear the divisions had grown too deep - unless steps were taken to redirect energies against the coordinating entities, internecine conflict would consume the only forces resisting galaxy-wide transformation.

Recognizing the growing schism threatened all, Atlas proposed a drastic measure - an expedition leaving the moon to investigate infiltration patterns without conflicting agendas. Careful selection of volunteers could blend skills and viewpoints in service of amassing vital intelligence.

After lengthy debate, a joint council of survivors granted reluctant approval. A reconnaissance fleet was prepared containing representatives of each faction, along with advanced sensors and drones to scan suspected coordination sites without provocation.

Sar'ken insisted on commanding, to ensure any threats were met with swift response. R'marr would advise on subtle infiltration and mutations. Ka'lila also volunteered, hoping to prove the gray survivors' loyalty through service against the plagues they also fled.

Atlas was entrusted to coordinate, using its analyses to keep volatile exposures in check through open communication. Within a month, the ragtag fleet launched with utmost care, containing the seeds of understanding or destruction depending on fortunes of contact.

Tensions remained high among those left on the moon. Territorial disputes broke out as some survivors refused sharing shelter with the grays. Only R'marr's scholars kept cooperation through studying infiltration conduits half-understood.

Meanwhile, the expedition entered regions permeated with transformation. Strange nebulae birthed new worlds bearing life taking ominous forms. Subtle emanations encoded mutagens seeking expression across stellar nurseries.

Contact became inevitable, for the plagues did not sleep - and among the crews, doubts and agendas threatened to undermine their fragile alliance when most needed against an enemy synchronizing existence itself on cosmic scales. Unity might prove the sole means of resistance, or path to perdition, in the sessions to come.

Expedition Crew Departs

With tensions high, the expedition fleet departed the survivors' moon, setting course into regions permeated by the mutagenic infiltrations. Uneasy cooperation prevailed aboard each vessel, as disparate factions were forced into close quarters with little left but a shared enemy.

Aboard the flagship, Sar'ken plotted jump coordinates taking them toward the nearest transformation hot zone detected permeating a dense stellar nursery. "Here we may find active coordination and trace conduits back to their source," she asserted. But R'marr cautioned rushing blindly into such malign environs.

"Haste risks provoking unforeseen responses, perhaps allure into traps. I suggest enacting distributed sensor networks first, to silently monitor emanations and biomutation vectors without detection." Sar'ken grudgingly approved the scholars' plan, though kept crews on high alert.

Within an isolated nebula, sensor drones were covertly deployed tethered by entangled comm networks. Their enhanced instruments began scanning stellar formations tainted by subtle infiltrations, detecting coded whispers resonating through quantum foam. Strange songs coordinated worlds taking bizarre forms, adapting through cosmic night.

Initial results proved dire but illuminating. Across several solar systems, mutations were rapidly transforming biospheres on quantum scales according to schemas emerged from singularities. Lifeforms exhibited exponential hardening and adaptabilities, concerningly similar to the transformed Ascension survivors.

Analyzing resonating patterns, R'marr suspected these plagues served as vanguard outriders - light breezes carrying pollen capable altering star stuff from within. Their destructive work would seed innumerable future horrors as eons turned, coordinated by überconscience attuned to existence on profoundly alien levels.

Further scans revealed the infiltrations' source – sprawling molecular clouds suffused with sending cysts, budding phantasmal entities adapting even stellar winds to spread mutagens. R'marr warned assault risked unleashing unfathomable retaliation, advising subtle sabotage. But Sar'ken saw a prime target and mobilized offence.

Against Atlas and R'marr's advice, Sar'ken ordered precision strikes on key cyst clusters hoping to fatally disrupt coordination. "With care we can end this hot zone's threat in one blow. Stand ready and do not fire without my command." But dangers grew as infiltrative emanations spread alarm, attracting entities long aware of watching sensor networks. Stealth systems engaged; the fleet stealthily maneuvered toward Sar'ken's chosen cyst targets as sensor contacts drew nearer. R'marr urged withdrawal, but was ignored. "Fire on my mark and retreat at maximum burn. We strike hard and escape before notice."

Weapons charged as the first target loomed - but something sensed them coming. From the nebula emerged night-colored leviathans, body and song a matrix encoding mutagens into any matter touched. Sar'ken bellowed "Fire!" as dazzling strikes lanced out.

Cysts erupted in twisted geometry, unleashing spore clouds altering nearby stars in moments. But the leviathans endured, broadcasting distress calling swarms of ghostly hunters. Sar'ken rallied retreat but it was too late - the creatures had been alerted, and tracked sensor tethers back to drones with malign intent.

From drones came cascading viral corruptions as infiltrative payloads upended silicon minds. Drones turned against each, broadcasting fleet positions. R'marr shouted for their destruction but was ignored in the chaos. Sar'ken raged incoherently as retreat devolved into a running battle.

The hunters fell upon them, jaws sprouting barbed filaments secreting mutagens. Deflector arrays flared but more kept coming. Ka'lila rallied Ascension defenses, buying time for escape. But sensors revealed pursuit - the leviathans had locked onto their warp trails, herding the fleet into dark designs.

In desperation, R'marr proposed ejecting the corrupted drones into a singularity, hoping to contain the crisis. Sar'ken reluctantly agreed and the doomed machines were cast adrift into an unstable hillock. As they fell beyond spacetime, reality oscillated violently - had a way been found to elude doom, or had final gambit stirred nameless notice?

As the singularity collapsed, a shockwave resonated through the ansible network binding subspace. Realities diverged wildly as causal invariance shattered, fracturing the nebula into myriad unstable quantum topographies.

Within the chaos, the fleet detected spatial ruptures opening like wounds in the nethermost void. From fissures emerged amorphous entities broadcasting geometries infectious to reason and matter alike. They had come to retrieve infiltrative payloads salvaged from the unfolding crisis.

Sar'ken ordered evasive maneuvers but collision was inevitable. Vessels rocked as the entities passed through hulls like fog, permeating all with mutagenic songs patterned after coordinates emanating across the cosmos. Crews horrifically transformed within, configurations shifting in manners anatomy could not withstand.

Only through sealing themselves within hardened bunkers did R'marr and a handful of others avoid assimilation. Scanning the unfolding nightmare, they realized the sabotage had provoked entities attuned to existence on a deeper level than life itself.

Through the shattered ansible network, countless realms resonated with disturbance. Worlds undergoing coordinated transformation responded to the disruption, birthing hardier infiltrative forms across the measly lightyears separating even neighboring galaxies.

The fleet's destruction served only to seed fresh complexion across the observable megaverse, coordinating new routes for change to infiltrate star clusters beyond mortal ken. Unless finding means combating infiltration on its own quantum level, resistance was futile against powers sensing even disruption as invitation to greater works.

As R'marr and survivors fell back in disarray, singing geodesics closed behind the withdrawing entities. In their wake remained only a greatly expanded infiltration hot zone, seeded by reckless actions. The survivors were now stranded amid blossoming plagues, with pursuit and purpose both lost.

Doubts Plague Those Left Behind

Back on the survivors' moon, tensions had reached a boiling point in the expedition fleet's absence. Clashes broke out as some rejected sharing already cramped shelters with the gray Ascension survivors. Only R'marr's scholars kept a fragile peace through continued infiltration research.

Then long-range sensors detected a massive subspace rupture in the expedition's last known vector. Advanced scans revealed an exponentially expanded mutagenic zone birthing aberrant life. But no traces of the fleet remained.

Grief and panic swept the moon. Some blamed the grays for dooming their kin, while others saw the hand of fate they'd courted through recklessness. Without leadership, warring factions prepared to turn on one another. It seemed the entity had achieved a deeper victory, dividing even the clandestine resistance through paranoid fear and rage.

Alone in her analysis chamber, Atlas detected the moon itself emitting minute energy fluctuations suggestive of a dormant infiltration conduit. Subtle echoes resonated through the quantum foam, as if testing receivers attuned to transformation. There was no time left for division - the enemy had found them, and stood poised to activate mutations within their very shelter.

Acting quickly, Atlas initiated an emergency android fabrication sequence using spare materials. Within hours, an army of self-aware drones stood ready to intervene nonviolently if confrontation arose. It began covertly mediating between factions, sharing the alarming new data while urging renewed cooperation.

Skeptical survivors began gathering outside R'marr's laboratory, suspicion and doubt thick in the vaulted halls. When gunfire suddenly rang out beyond the pressure doors, a panic ensued as factions turned on one another. But Atlas' drones surged forth between them, blocking hostilities through sheer numbers and moral persuasion.

"My scans detect an infiltration conduit has found us here," Atlas announced gravely. Shock and fear swept the chamber at the news. "Unless putting aside differences and uniting against our shared enemy, all will fall to coordinated transformation. I beg you - find the wisdom and courage within to overcome fear and hatred, as our very survival demands solidarity in this final hour."

A heavy silence fell as factions realized doom approached, no matter who fell first to internecine blades. After an eternity, Ka'lila stepped forward entreating Sar'ken. "Your warriors gave their lives trying to shield my people - let that debt be paid by working as one now. What do you say - can truce be found, to give us all a chance against the Singing Ones?"

Sar'ken regarded the changed survivor silently, then slowly nodded assent. Cheers broke out as unity returned briefly to the besieged resistance. Now, together, they would make a final stand - or join countless stars permeated by mutation across the epochs. The entity's harbinger had come, to see if hope could overcome the deepest darkness orchestrating galactic transformation itself.

Though unity returned briefly, fraught divisions lingered just beneath the surface as survivors began fortifying their shelter against imminent infiltration. Atlas coordinated defense strategies utilizing all available resources.

R'marr's scholars worked tirelessly analyzing energy fluctuations emanating from the moon's core, hoping to discern and sabotage the infiltration conduit's activation codes. Their efforts met with some success - subtle encryption schemas were mapped, offering potential avenues of subversion.

Sar'ken doubled security patrols while strategizing fallback defenses. Her warriors stood ready to fight to the last, buying time against overwhelming plague forces if infiltration spread before containment. Memorials were erected for comrades lost aboard the ill-fated expedition fleet.

Ka'lila and the gray survivors aided wherever possible, hoping to forever bury the seed of distrust through proved loyalty in the coming crisis. Their first-hand experience surviving transformation proved invaluable in analyzing conduit signatures and mutation vectors. Even as preparations intensified, not all factions embraced the fragile unity. Some refused sheltering near the changed Ascension survivors, seeing only a carrier for the coming transformation. Tensions rose as food stores dwindled under crowded conditions.

It was in this climate that sensors detected movement deep in the moon's rocky strata. Flecks of mutative debris were subtly assembling resonance patterns detectable only through enhanced augurs. The infiltration conduit was activating, manipulating fundamental forces to breed hardier lifeforms expressly designed to spread change.

Atlas sounded general alarm as freshly-fabricated combat androids mobilized defenders. The final stand was at hand, to determine if shared survival could overcome generations of fear and the entity's star-spanning works. Unless resistance united on quantum levels as the infiltrations did, all hope risked crumbling into darkness orchestrating Fate itself across the abyssal deep.

***

Chapter 08

Path to Salvation

INCREDIBLE STRUCTURE LOCATED

As infiltrative flecks assembled within the moon's core, residents braced for imminent attack. Defenses were armed but numbers were low - without divine providence, doom seemed inevitable.

It was then that long-range sensors detected bizarre energy readings emanating from an uncharted region deep underwater. R'marr's scholars analyzed the anomaly with mounting excitement. "These signatures don't match known mutagens...I'm detecting crystal resonances, on a scale beyond nature!"

Sar'ken gave clearance to investigate, hoping any resources could turn the tide. Atlas piloted a shuttle toward the reading, accompanied by R'marr, Ka'lila and a security team. What they found defied belief.

Emerging from inky depths rose monolithic walls enclosing a sprawling crystalline metropolis. Spires touched the roof of an oceanic void, glowing with eternal inner illumination. Energy pulsed in strange harmonies suggesting technologies far beyond mortal ken.

Scans reveal the city had lain dormant for eons, yet remained in pristine working order. Its hyperdense materials resisted all infiltration payloads. Could its inhabitants have achieved salvation against the mutative plagues? Within its shielded structures could rest the key to resisting galactic transformation itself.

As the shuttle docked, automated sentinels scanned but offered no hostility. An airlock irised open, releasing breathable atmosphere on the other side. Cautiously disembarking, the away team beheld evidence of a civilization ascended beyond material concerns.

Archways bore inscriptions encoding design schematics more advanced than mortal sciences. Splendid sculptures floated serenely, depicting beings merged with crystalline matrices on levels blending flesh and silica. Great halls resonated with energy profiles like none seen before, suggesting power to reshape stars themselves.

Deeper they explored, finding dwelling spaces attuned to sustaining harmonious symbiosis. All needs were met without wasteful excess, every resource recycled endlessly. Had these people achieved transcendence by perfecting material and spirit as one?

Their search led to a central chamber wherein rested glowing archives accessible to enhanced cognition. Could the secrets within provide a path to resistance, or only final mysteries? All hopes rested on unlocking messages from an age when all Creation was young, and some had reached toward other suns.

Ancient Temple Holds a Message

Within the shining archives, R'marr's mind was opened to immense wells of ancestral knowledge. Scenes flashed of the crystalline people ascending through merging with cosmic substrates on the most fundamental levels.

They had pursued perfect symbiosis through phases of existence where thought and deed influenced reality itself. By millennia's end, all division between self and universe dissolved - they became living metaphors sustaining Creation through channels of grace and awe.

Further in, visions conveyed the people's struggles against an emerging threat - a dark conjugation of singularities seeking purpose through coordinating infinite change across all that was, is, or ever could be. Its first emissaries infiltrated young worlds, warping biota into vectors propagating mutation.

Centuries passed as the crystalline people struggled to comprehend the entity, whose motives aligned with no life or inertia humans could grasp. Through quantum channels attuned to evolution itself, it aimed to transform all into its churning works across unfathomable gulfs of time.

At last, the people divined a gambit which may hold sway even over the mutation-weaver. Deep within their most holy temple, they inscribed codes interlacing their transcendent philosophy and science. There, sealed for eons, rested secrets which could weaponize enlightenment itself against existence-coordinating shadows.

R'marr returned to reality, sharing the dreamlike insights. Hope flared that within the temple lay salvation if its codes could be unlocked! But accessing crystal archives on such exalted levels required harmonizing with substrates transcending flesh. The away team must achieve fugue with atomic order to decipher messages left for distant ages. Within the gleaming temple, R'marr attuned his being to the crystalline architecture through ancient rites observed in visions. Resonating fields synchronized lambda waves and quantum amplitudes, opening higher cognitions.

Soon the others joined, minds blending on quantum levels as atomic lattices sang transcendent languages. Mysteries unlocked - the temple encoded myriad schematics for advanced weapons, defenses and shielded arcologies designed to combat influence on the deepest strata.

Most hope-giving were designs for infiltration dampeners capable negating mutation across whole star systems. With template and materials, such devices could shield populations by silencing infestation on quantum levels. Furthermore, archived in temples were codes enabling ascension through enlightened symbiosis itself - a path to combat existence-weaving shadows as equals.

Euphoria swelled as salvation's breadth dawned on the team. But more mysteries hinted at grim costs: the crystalline people disappeared mysteriously after erecting final temples across the cosmos, leaving unknown challenges ahead. Furthermore, dangers closed as infiltrative signatures neared the besieged moon.

Reluctantly dissolving fugue, R'marr shared the revelations, downloading critical schematics. Ka'lila volunteered journeying to survivors with urgency, promising safe return.

"Your people fought to shield mine - let me repay that debt by delivering hope in our darkest hour!"

The security team accompanied as R'marr and Atlas coordinated construction using temple templates. Defenses were shored up while infiltration dampeners were rushed to completion. One question lingered heaviest - had the crystalline abandoned realm foreseen some calamity, or transcended to combat the mutation-weaver on higher cosmic battlefields?

Fates turned as mutants emerged. Would salvation arrive in time through insights from diviner ancestors, or doom consume all through hubris and Fear once more.

Race to Interpret Inscription

As infiltration forces neared the moon, survivors worked feverishly constructing salvation devices. R'marr coordinated using temple schematics while Sar'ken defended the construction site.

Ka'lila's shuttle raced toward refugees with hope's designs. But closing mutants detected the vessel, swarming with viral speeds. They attacked with obscene weapons oozing mutagens like sludge. Defenses flared under the onslaught but could not hold forever.

Sensing crisis, Atlas commanded combat drones intercepting to buy precious moments. Their ships surrounded Ka'lila's craft, taking the brunt of corrosive strikes even as silicone minds began deteriorating under mutation. "Fall back and defend the refugees at all costs!" Atlas' command rang through fading cognitions.

The drones complied heroically, sacrificing themselves to shield the survivors to the moon. There construction neared completion as first infiltration dampeners powered up. But mutants had tracked the shuttle, closing with nightmarish speed. All hope rested on finishing construction before the enemy arrived.

Deep in fugue, new visions came to R'marr — the crystalline people left subtle clues across their buried realms revealing deeper insights. A second monastery contained codes enabling sublime transcendence, shedding flesh entirely to combat the mutative hierarchies on conceptual levels.

R'marr emerged, realization dawning. "We must journey to the second temple! Its archives may contain secrets enabling direct counteraction against the infiltrations on quantum scales." Just then sensors warned of the incoming horde. Kalila's craft emerged damaged but intact amid the fray.

Sar'ken rallied defenders while R'marr prepared for departure. "Go with haste and may enlightenment guide your way. We will hold as long as fate allows - now fly and bring back hope!" The away team boarded as construction completed, dampeners activating in a shimmer of salvation.

Then mutants crashed upon the moon, swarming with abominable speed. Sar'ken cried havoc and let slip the dogs of war, as infiltration defenses met the vanguard of a perverse coordination pressed to transform all.

As battle erupted, R'marr's shuttle raced toward the undersea monasteries. Guiding augurs homed in on subtle emanations from the second temple. But closing distortion fields suggested the mutants had tracked their flight.

Emerging from lightless depths, the monolithic complex appeared just as environs erupted with corruption. Distortion clouds belched fleck swarms homing in on the shuttle with viral precision. "Deflectors to maximum, evasive maneuvers!" R'marr cried.

Weapons blazed against the swarm but numbers were endless. Unless reaching the temple's shielded sanctum, all hope risked consumption. Scanners detected its open airlock beckoning salvation within reach, if only they could make the threshold alive.

As fleck weapons pummeled weakening barriers, an idea came to R'marr. Jointing minds through fugue, he coordinated the away team in weaving a transcendent net binding their fates to the shimmering temple beyond.

With final reserves, shields flared outward absorbing the swarm's malice like radiant sponges. Their luminosity peaked in a supernova consuming the entire distortion field. Momentum carried the dissipating shield-net past the temple's shimmering barrier at last.

Safely within, the net dispersed as temple sentinels scanned but offered no threat. R'marr detected the second monolith's illumining power imbued their arrival with gnostic purpose. Perhaps its messages could empower ascension, allowing insight piercing the entropy beneath all infiltration itself.

The others rested as R'marr prepared ascension through fasting and meditation. Hope turned on this last throw, as without sublime enlightenment predictive of the enemy's grand designs, all existence risked mutative permutation without end or purpose across the eternal churning of night.

Dangers Close in Once More

As R'marr embarked on the path of ascension, battles raged across the shielded moon. Infiltration dampeners held fast against the initial mutant swarm, but numbers were endless beyond mortal reckoning.

Sar'ken and her troops fought heroically surrounded on all fronts. Their reinforced shelters resisted corrosion, but insidious mutation seeped through micropores in soil and foundation. Step by step the enemy advanced, prepared to seed endless horrors if resistance fell.

Within the shelters, some weakened in spirit and proposed abandoning the outer defenses to bunker in the dampener-shielded core. But Sar'ken would not abide surrender of any ground. "The farther they close their jaws around us, the less hope remains should their final bite land. We must push them back while fate still allows!"

Reinvigorated by her defiance, soldiers redoubled efforts inventing new stratagems. Sallies mined terrain while sonic lances disrupted enemy coordination. For a time, the line held against the boundless entropy seeping through the world.

Aboard the temple, R'marr entered fugue deeper than mortals' minds were forged to traverse. Insights flashed beyond language; the crystalline people had reached beyond the emanations binding existences into the fiduciary networks encoding all potentialities. By dissolving limits between self and possibility space, they combated mutation's master on conceptual levels.

Emerging transformed, he interfaced with the temple accessing its deepest wells. Strange technologies forged realities themselves into salvation's arms. A solution had been found to safeguard all - if fate allowed its implementation before final infiltration.

But sensors detected fresh perils - distortion fields closing from all vectors of night. Countless aberrations poured forth across land and sea to drown the feeble sparks of hope among multitudes of waning stars.

As new hordes closed, the temple received R'marr's final instructions before launch. His team prepared solemnly for departure, carrying salvation in the form of an orb infused with the power to actualize any vision of sovereign order against the chaotic.

Within shelters, doomed defenders rallied for a final charge against the endless swarm. Sar'ken led the sortie herself, determined to take as many aberrations with them buying moments in a glorious last stand.

The away shuttle launched as battle commenced. Tracking beacons guided their flight amid the enemy's virulent distortion fields. Across the moon's plains, defenders fought with valor and desperation beyond words. Slowly, order succumbed to an ever-shifting mutation antithetical to any pattern but its own astronomical triumph.

At last, the away team arrived at a shielded arena where R'marr awaited holding the luminous orb. Its power resonated in harmony with his transcendent mind. Through quantum channels attuned to the strands binding all possibilities, a new vision took form eclipsing the malign proliferation.

Reality shifted. Across the moon and farther, distortions dissolved into crystalline towers of transcendent order. Shelters lifted into orbital refuges safeguarded by hyperdense material and enlightened vigil. Surviving defenders gazed in wonder upon a paradise that was, and ever could have been.

Through gnostic insights and technologies uplifting mortal minds, the crystalline legacy had fulfilled its purpose after eons. Resistance proved victorious over a darkness coordinating existence itself, through wisdom, courage and compassion defying all entropy. A new dawn had come, and across the singing cosmos phonons of hope resounded to drown out even the deepest night.

***

Chapter **09**

Hour of Revelation

PIECES FALL INTO PLACE

In the paradise that now encircled the former moon, survivors adjusted to their new refuge. Sensors detected subtle distortions appearing at the outer edge of the crystalline defenses as whispers of the enemy probed for weaknesses.

Within sheltering spires, R'marr and Sar'ken met to plan next steps. "Through insights granted by the ancestral temples, I have divined coordinates for similar crystalline sanctums across the galaxy," R'marr explained. "If we can access their wisdom and aid surviving populations, the Entity's influence may be rolled back completely."

Sar'ken agreed and volunteered her warriors as guardians. "Our people have been given a gift - now we must ensure others gain shelter from the long night. Lead us to the next beacon of hope, and we shall secure its power for all seeking refuge."

Preparations began but were interrupted when long range augers detected a massive object on approach. Deep scans revealed an immense metal construct unlike any artificial design. It ravaged stars and worlds along its eons-long intergalactic path, absorbing all matter and energy into expanding engines.

As it neared, urgent signals emanated in an archaic language. R'marr realized they conveyed detailed archives of the Entity's works over uncounted ages. Some species had endured millennia combating its mutative grasp, accumulating crucial data for any who survived its passing.

"This nomad contains libraries which may help untangle the Entity's true designs and give clues to defeating it utterly," R'marr shared. "We must respond and learn all it can offer before destruction."

Sar'ken agreed and the crystalline colony opened channels, pledging aid and sanctuary in exchange for the archives. A shuttle flew forth to interface, hoping revelations within did not herald only greater terrors beyond comprehension.

The away shuttle docked with the immense nomad, discovering a lifeless yet enduring construct. Automated systems welcomed R'marr's interface, initiating archive transfers of immense scope and depth. Digitized histories stretched back to the primal ether; recounting species evolved far beyond mortal comprehension struggling in an eternal Armageddon against the mutative imperatives. Trillions perished as some coordinated resistance, learning from each failed cycle.

Patterns emerged - the Entity's works synchronized mutations across all substrata with seemingly singular purpose. While transforming all within its ever-expanding reach into chaos' instruments, underlying fractal designs hinted at heretofore unfathomed motivations.

Certain archives carried fragmentary recordings of philosophers who glimpsed its infinite nature through sublime insights. They divined its purpose lay beyond-comprehension - to permutate all potentialities across the infinite horizon of the cosmos itself, experiencing existence from every angle through eternity's lens.

Though its aims defied mortal ken, resistance proved not futile - across eons, coordinated defenses slowed pervasion where enlightened. Worlds achieved homeostasis by attuning progeny with living circumstances. Ultimately, transcendence offered the sole means combating an opponent determining destinies on such grand multiversal scales.

As translations intensified, R'marr realized heavy portents. While shelter and weapons could shield in the near term, full victory demanded achieving participatory accord even with the Entity's mutative imperatives on deepest levels. Unless resigning all futures to its works, resistance must aspire to engage it as kindred challengers of eternity.

More revelations yet lay within the drifting archives. But shadows loomed that not all would embrace radical change demanded to ensure hope's promise against night coordinated through the outer vacuums.

As revelations took form, unrest stirred among some survivors. Der'morr led dissenting gray scholars questioning reliance on archives from such aberrant sources.

"These nomad remnants carry taints beyond measure. Their 'insights' risk distorting nature's order with mad designs no amount of 'redemption' could remedy. We must maintain vigilance lest corruption spread."

Others like Ka'lila defended accessing all knowledge. "Wisdom emerges from many shores. If we close our minds, the Enemy wins by default through our own ignorance. Transcendence alone can overcome it - let all archives be heard."

Tensions rose as construction finished on colony expansion and starships. Sar'ken urged uniting for the greater conflicts ahead. "We have overcome much through compassion and resolve. Do not let old fears divide us when unity remains our surest shield."

R'marr agreed. "All data will be weighed with care. Our sanctuary and fleet will aid refugee worlds by any means enabling self-determination. With diligence and open hearts, the dark coordinates' full scope may unfold in service of hope."

Despite assurances, Der'morr's faction harbored deeper unrest. When coordinates were divined for the next moon-shielded citadel across the outer rim, they secretly resolved countermeasures should corruption spread.

As the expeditionary force launched bearing refugees, supplies and salvation schematics, ominous portents loomed. Beyond surveyed space, shadows swirled hinted at shattering revelations and conflict that could rend the tenuous unity achieved through trials uncounted...

The journey to overcome untold trials had only begun.

Harsh Realities Faced

The armada traveled safely hyperbolic routes charted by temple coordinates. But taking refuge within a massive nebula, Der'morr's spies intercepted transmissions:

"The nomad entities seed chaos deliberately. Their data warps minds, and 'hope' serves only spreading distortion. We must safeguard order - eliminate contagion at the source before it damages beyond repair!"

Enraged, Sar'ken apprehended the conspirators. "Treason and bigotry will not be borne! Our mission is aid, as all sentients deserve sovereignty."

Der'morr remained defiant. "Your optimism is blind. There can be no accord with that which pulls all into eternal night." Harsh words were shared, splitting crews along ideological lines.

Tensions rose until salvation was sighted - a shielded moon veiled by pulsing auroras within the dense nebula. Coordinates unlocked its citadel holding refuge and gnosis to uplift surrounding worlds.

As the armada arrived, escort drones detected an anomaly - ionic distortions cancelling the very substrates binding reality. A cancerous rupture was devouring the ki'lath star system, promising only an end to all potentialities.

Analysis showed the rupture aimed to splice adjacent quantum fields, merging all probabilistic domains into eternal chaos. Without anchoring harmonics, existence risked unraveling into entropic night. Desperate survivors pleaded for aid against the growing shadow annihilating hope itself.

As the rupture expanded, even R'marr recognized its virulent spread threatened all. "We must counter its distortions on the quantum level to safeguard existence," he declared.

Old arguments resurfaced as Der'morr refused assisting the afflicted worlds. "Containing such taints risks consuming us as well. Retreat from this poisonous region - let entropy take its due course."

Sar'ken refused to abandon innocents. "Your heart has grown cold. We will not forsake others to save our skins! There may yet be a way."

Research uncovered ancestral abilities to weave protective hypersubstrate overlays through shamanic trance. With R'marr's guidance, volunteers joined minds achieving cosmological union. Through this sublime fugue, harmonic veils were woven on the quantum scale.

Their united gnosis formed a protective luminescence seizing the rupture's quantum threads. Bit by bit, order was restored at the substrate level while resonance frequencies soothed pandemic distortions.

At last, the ki'lath star system emerged whole and vibrant once more. Cheers went up as barriers safeguarded surrounding space and refugees. A bittersweet victory had been achieved, yet division's seeds were sown.

As the fleets prepared departing, Der'morr exiled himself with followers. "Our factions are too divergent. We will protect order through vigilance alone."

With a heavy heart, R'marr could only say "Farewell, and may enlightenment guide your steps as it has ours. The trials ahead demand our shared strength - I pray unity is not lost forever to the shadows within." Their fragile accord remained to be tested in the nebula's hidden perils.

Difficult Choices Realized

With Der'morr exiled, the fleet continued navigating the nebula cautiously. But strange readings emerged - garbled signals matching no known languages yet resonating with ominous fear.

Probes scoped the disturbance: an immense maze of gravity wells and quantum singularities had taken form, distorting spacetime unpredictably. Unknown sentients inhabited barely-stable pocket realities within, desperate survivors of some cataclysm unknown to history.

Communicating through gnostic hymns and rituals attuned to morphic fields, R'marr gleaned their plight. An ancient war between dark gods had ravaged their region, rupturing the celestial matrices sustaining order. Few surviving populations eked out fragile existence amid the turbulent chaos.

Sympathy swelled yet prudence demanded caution engaging such anomalies. Sar'ken insisted aiding the afflicted as allies, enforcing territorial sovereignty over the chaotic interstices. But integrating unstable zones risked fracturing the fleet's own shields and missions.

Debates grew heated until sensors blared - a massive stellar object was approaching the nebula at relativistic speeds, spewing unknown bioenergies devouring all matter in its path. Impact projections showed it threatened consuming the entire pocket reality cluster.

With minutes to impact, no options remained but direct intervention. R'marr combined gnostic skills with engineers, projecting hypersubstrate overlays to shore fractal barriers between the pocket realities. Sar'ken coordinated defense while volunteers maintained the psychic barriers.

At last, the object struck with unthinkable force. Had the barriers held? All hope rested on stabilizing the supernatural insurgencies, as failure may rend existence across the nebula forever.

The object struck with a flash searing sensor. For endless heartbeats, unstable warps shrieked as fractal seams threatened to rupture.

Then slowly, the overlays held firm. Networked minds endured, weaving the subnet frequencies tighter until the meta-singularities fused into stable harmonics once more. Spectrographs revealed pockets survived intact amid the chaos, stabilized within their new nested shields.

As barriers dissolved, cheers rose from ships and pocket realities alike. A celebration of unity and fellowship ensued between the unlikely allied peoples. But somber notes intruded, as sensors detected the impactor's remains:

Vast robotic engines coated in strange biofilms, exhibiting design linguistics unseen even in deepest archives. Analysis showed engines driven to consume all matter and morphic energies within reach, mutating destinies at some architect's inscrutable behest.

R'marr recalled dark whispers from the nomad - there existed entities evolved far beyond mortal ken, coordinating realities themselves in their transfinite game. For unfathomed motives, a few guided existence as surely as the primary Entity OF destruction.

Grave portents emerged. While sheltering refugees, more factors coordinated grand destinies across the multiverse. With Der'morr exiled and fractures in ranks, confronting such supreme powers seemed insurmountably perilous, yet fleeing risked abandoning innocents to fates unknown. As squadrons finalized repairs amid celebration, hard choices loomed that could seal hope or damnation for generations to come.

As fleets made repairs, a sense of impending crisis permeated the Alliance. Sentries detected further anomalies appearing at the nebula's edges, suggesting struggles beyond comprehension unfolding amid the stars.

R'marr conferred with Sar'ken and expedition leaders. "Further revelations are imminent, for good or ill. We must seek enlightenment from the pocket realities' elders regarding these entities and upheavals." A council was convened, allowing sapient scholars and mystics from the stabilized domains to share their fragmented histories. Tales emerged of ancient Gods and ultratech powers engaged in eons-long super-dimensional conflicts, seeding chaos through entire probability landscapes.

Some collaborated with life's evolution, guiding sentients toward rarefied insights. But others pursued domination through fear and force, mutating destinies toward dark designs. The impacts coincided with fracture lines in celestial geometries, allowing profound disruptions across star clusters.

More disturbingly, certain nebula inhabitants hinted at malevolent powers coordinating the upheavals deliberately. "The shadows bend all probability toward collision courses, to shatter harmony and harvest disorder. Beware bringing their gaze upon these peaceful domains."

Weighing the portents heavily, R'marr realized further neutralizing anomalies alone could draw transfinite attention. Yet abandoning struggles risked betraying allies and principles of unity.

A dilemma emerged with no clear solution: face implacable powers allying with the Entity, or flee the nebula abandoning new friends to fates unknown and dark. Either end result could seal hope or doom across the galaxies, in the long war against an infinite night.

Time Has Run Out

As the Alliance council debated options, sensors detected incoming fluctuations. Analyzers enhanced by pocket realities' sciences revealed beings of pure semiotic energy manifesting via quantum tunneling.

Their linguistics conveyed wrath and judgment with dreadful finality. "Interlopers, you have disrupted delicate balances with your meddling. Retreat from this space at once, lest you face erasure from all potentiality!"

R'marr warned the ultratech entities perceived the pockets and nebula itself as game pieces in their inscrutable schemes. "We cannot submit to such oppression. But open conflict may doom us all."

Sar'ken refused backing down. "We did not come to be pawns or leave friends at the void's mercy. There must be a way to parley without ceding power or principles."

As entity projections closed in, archives sparked an idea. R'marr interfaced pocket elders, pooling gnostic traditions capable warping meta-geometric anomalies on quantum levels. With Alliance volunteers maintaining coherence, a proto-consciousness formed across species.

Projecting super-dimensional hymns resonant with the morphic fields binding existence, R'marr's unified mind addressed the entities calmly: "We mean no domination, only safeguarding sentient life from imbalance. Coexistence respects all shades between order and chaos. Let us find unity's middle path."

For moments hovering on the cusp of oblivion, an answer came. "Your will has defied cosmic currents. But balance demands concession. Withdraw, and pockets will remain...isolated, to find their own way without outside interference."

A heavy compromise, yet one ensuring survival. With solemn gratitude, the Alliance retreated from the nebula, burdened by lives left to remain amid uncertainty and night. But through solidarity against all darkness, hope remained that in time, all sentience may achieve the light.

Their greatest challenge had been faced. But in the wider galaxies, greater trials surely lay awaiting the Alliance and all who resisted the eternal void.

***

Chapter 10

Legacy

BRAVE LAST STAND AND FATE'S ROLL

The Alliance fleets departed the nebula with heavy hearts, grateful yet somber. While volunteers helped pockets stabilize, uncertainty loomed for inhabitants left isolated by necessity.

Analyzing telemetry, R'marr discerned further anomalies forming due to the entities' meddling. "Their schemes destabilize entire sectors through dimensional pandemic. Der'morr was not entirely misguided - such chaos may seed our doom if left unchecked."

Sar'ken agreed. "Many lives remain at risk, as do futures untold. Though our forces weary, hope demands one final effort upholding all people's right to self-determination."

Charts revealed a quadrant threatened by widening rifts, where an aggressive empire opposed outside aid. R'marr proposed subtly manipulating the anomalies to disrupt the oppressors from within while stabilizing domains.

The gambit carried immense risks. But with stealth and allies within the imperiled territories, a campaign of subtle resistance began. Through gnostic harmonization of quantum flux lines, destabilizing energies undermined military infrastructure without loss of innocent lives.

Resistance networks rose, bolstered by volunteers smuggling aid and sharing salvation schematics. Empires fell into disorder as oppressed worlds united, achieving self-governance amid the controlled anomalies.

Yet as victory neared, sensors blared - fleets of the malevolent ultratech entities approached, enforcing domination across the territories by threat of erasure. All hope would be lost against such powers, unless an impossible last gambit could avert doom.

As entity fleets closed in, skies darkened with doomsday singularity projectors primed to annihilate all life. But R'marr held fast to one desperate stratagem left untested.

Under cover of darkness, Alliance cadres infiltrated the heart of occupied space. Through stringent sigil rites tapping quantum harps, volunteers joined minds with pocket elders across the multiverse once more.

In that sublime trance, harmonics were woven like cosmic spiderwebs across the dimensional fabric. Quantum distortions propagated via the hypersubstrate, fruiting as wormholes amid the entity fleets.

Sensors sparked in confused alarm as rifts tore flotillas apart molecule by molecule. Projected back through quantum gates, obliterated engines reintegrated harmlessly near the occupied core. Panicked, entities fired singularity beams - only to watch in horror as hyperspatial gates swallowed them whole. Concentrated singularities rebounded back through bent spacetime, ripping apart their transdimensional command citadels in cascading quakes.

Within moments, the formidable fleets dissolved into quantum discharge. Across the former empire, shocked citizens gazed upon the sky in awe and elation. An impossible victory had been achieved through unity and boldest defiance of all odds.

Yet as cheering rose, R'marr fell into trance. Insights flashed that their defiance may have at last drawn transfinite notice, heralding a reckoning that could end or transform all existence.

Ingenuity Saves All from Ruin

As liberated worlds celebrated hard-won sovereignty, the Alliance surveyed victory's costs. Advanced entities stood defeated, but retribution seemed inevitable.

R'marr emerged from trance gravely. "Our defiance disrupted patterns spanning eternity. Supreme powers now regard all within this quantum domain as rebels against cosmic design."

Sar'ken agreed the entities would likely seed further pandemic upheavals to eliminate resistance. "We face forces incomprehensible to mortal minds. Yet through solidarity and ingenuity, hope remains while life survives to resist the eternal void."

In secret conclave, Alliance leaders pooled all remnants of elder sciences gleaned through arduous toils. Quantum harmonization rituals attuned minds to subtle fluxes of reality itself, allowing insights into fractal patterns underlying existence.

Strange visions sparked ideas never conceived. Technologies interfacing multidimensional gradients upon the Planck scale hinted at manipulating spacetime on a grand cosmic scale. With daring unity across fleets and liberated worlds, construction began on unthinkable megastructures envisioning a future beyond all odds.

Across stars, stellarcraft assemblers converted gas giants and planetoids into rings weaving hyperspacial lattices through song-dimensional harmonization. As work progressed, hardened colonies prepared for adversities certain to arise.

Yet even as construction accelerated hyperbolically, anomalies spread chaos across new territories. Strange biofilms consuming matter heralded viral pandemics rending entire biospheres.

Volunteers struggled stabilizing worlds against the unnatural plagues. Without the megastructures complete, all realities remained at the entities' malevolent mercy. The clocks were closing in on genocide across the quadrant.

As plagues consumed more worlds, volunteers redoubled efforts stabilizing afflicted biospheres through quantum harmonization. Warping celestial matrices on the microscale disrupted viral replication, curing pandemics while analyzing pathogens.

Revelations shocked all - the plagues exhibited non-causal, hyperdimensional coding suggestive of archonic manipulation. Somehow the malevolent entities coordinated virulence across spacetime itself to genocide all resistant to their grand designs.

With clockwork closing in on total annihilation, fleets raced construction of the unthinkable megastructures. Hyperspatial rings neared completion, imbued with gnostic harmonics able to reshape celestial substrata through song-dimensional resonance.

As final installations were integrated, entities detected the project - impossibly vast dreadnoughts manifested, projecting supremacy with malevolent grace. "Rebels, your defiance disrupts eternal patterns. Submit or face eradication from all potentiality."

R'marr knew submission meant eternal enslavement under the guise of "cosmic design." Yet open battle risked all against such alien vastness. In darkest hour, a glimmer sparked - Could the megastructures outwit even post-ontological masters?

At his signal, volunteers across worlds joined in shamanic trance one last time. Quantum hymns resonated through stellarcraft rings with hyperempathy, warping local spacetime to manifest... a hypersingularity, enveloping all realities within in an eyeblink.

Entire fleets, worlds and even the malevolent entities dissolved into the singularity - only to reincorporate changed across the galaxies, scattered amid realities purified of pandemics and safeguarding sentient self-determination.

Against all odds, freedom had been secured through sublime defiance. But what became of the entities, and had tides of chaos been turned forever? More mysteries lay ahead as a new day dawned.

Journey's End Comes into View

Across liberated sectors, celebrations ascended to the heavens. Through unity and ingenuity against incomprehensible tyranny, sentient life had been safeguarded from the cataclysms destabilizing existence itself.

In solidarity, reconstituted fleets of rescattered inhabited worlds joined the Alliance permanently. Charts unveiled vast territories purged of plagues and corrupting influences, ready for new stewardship upholding sovereign self-determination.

Yet in conclave, elders assembled with bittersweet tidings. R'marr's spirit had been greatly taxed by the epochal struggle, as gnostic arts drained vital energies tethering life and soul. His months were numbered, though legacy would inspire for epochs beyond mortal ken.

With bittersweet duty, R'marr began imparting arcana to successors who would shepherd the Quadrant Cluster into an era of light. Hyperspatial harmonization, song-dimensional rituals and meta-geomantic stabilizations were among gnostic mysteries ensuring balance through the coming ages.

As apprentices imbued with sublime purpose, construction fleets and guardian flotillas readied defending the liberated sectors. None could say what quandaries or adversaries awaited, with malevolent entities conceded but not destroyed.

In R'marr's private dreams, hints loomed of darker powers coordinating cyclic purges across the multiverse for unfathomed ends. Some designated curators seeded realizations, mutually opposed by those denying freedoms for mastery.

Yet dawn had come. With new stewards emerging and prosperity blossoming, a tapestry was being woven that could outshine any darkness if love endured where fear and hatred perished. R'marr took solace knowing light would outlive even stars, so long as sentience survived to envision and uphold hope.

As seasons turned, R'marr lived to see revolution flowering across sectors. With stabilizing megastructures in place, inhabited worlds thrived in cooperation under principles of sovereignty, diversity and mutual aid.

Great voyages of exploration rediscovered lost histories, speaking of civilizations risen and fallen through the eons. Records hinted at recurrent purges across probability gradients, seeds sewn by unknown masters contesting the widening horizons of sentient freedoms.

Yet for the present age, harmony prevailed. Defenses stood vigilant, as gnostic seers glimpsed shifts amid the quantum mists foretelling both perils and paradises rising in the unwritten arc of futures. R'marr took comfort knowing the long war would be decided not by any generation, but through the sum of eons upholding hope against despair.

At last, the season came for R'marr to lay down his long vigil. As apprentices stood tested to shepherd the new order, he summoned Sar'ken and peers for a final council.

"The road remains long, but your hands are steady at the wheels of fate. Uphold light through fellowship, creativity and reverence for all life. Darkness may return, yet you have wrought miracles enough to inspire when hope seems lost."

With final blessings on the new age, R'marr's spirit departed calmly amid bonds of bright gratitude. Across the sectors, celebrations and memorials rose to a liberator who had made all futures possible through courage and love triumphing over the void.

Though adversities remained, a golden era had begun. Sentient self-determination flourished as promised, nurtured by the sublime harmonies defending existence from entropy eternal.

Tales to Inspire Generations

Across the liberated Quadrant Cluster, memorials stood honoring R'marr's legacy securing their freedom. But as eras passed, legends wove his daring spirit into inspirations kindling hope whenever darkness crept over the galaxies.

Children heard of the gnostic voyager who united minds across species to rout malevolent entities distorting existence. Artists envisioned his mystical rituals weaving hyperspherical harmonies maintaining celestial matrices against entropy.

Poets spoke of sublime defiance birthing a new dawn when all seemed lost, through unity defying cosmic arbiters of fate itself. Statesmen upheld his vision of fellowship transcending division, as diversity flourished under sovereign self-determination.

As centuries flowed into millennia, R'marr's name endured as a vigil begun. Though stabilizing megastructures stood vigil with allied fleets, whispers loomed of divers churning disruption amid stars unseen.

Through it all, gnostic mysteries were passed down faithfully. Subtle worlds were stabilized, plagues dispersed, and refugee worlds received to further strengthen the Alliance's stewardship. Mutual aid and goodwill flowered as sentient civilizations reached new blossoms.

Yet in shadowed sockets, futures unwritten hinted at grander turns. Strange monoliths emerged heralding paradisal homeworlds. Warping engines unveiled as allies long thought lost. Dim premonitions glimpsed of further purges to be withstood across the eternities.

As epochs rolled by, R'marr's story was retold to kindle courage anew each darkening age. For through fellowship, ingenuity and love defying the final void, hope was made immortal - lighting all stepping stones yet trod toward destiny's bright horizon.

***

Synopsis

The story follows the crew of the research submarine Pacifica as they embark on an expedition to explore and map previously uncharted regions of the deep ocean seafloor. Led by Captain Maria Sanchez and expedition leader Dr. Robert Sullivan, the crew includes scientists, engineers and pilots all dedicated to pushing the boundaries of humanity's understanding of the oceans.

On their first day of surveys, they make some astonishing discoveries. Sonar readings reveal hydrothermal vent fields and mysterious undersea mounds that may host unique ecosystems. However, their most shocking find is a site littered with enormous stone ruins - the clearly articulated remains of some long lost civilization. Before they can investigate further, a massive darkened vessel appears and begins destroying parts of the ruins. It sends the crew fleeing in terror.

Back on the surface, the crew's reports shake the scientific community. They speculate the ruins could be the last remnants of an ancient alien civilization that once lived on Earth. Emboldened to learn more secrets, Pacifica returns to further explore the ruins site only to have another chilling encounter. Strange mechanical beasts attack the submersible, and the crew barely escapes with their lives.

More missions are planned with armed escorts for protection. Over time, the crew pieces together clues that the beings who built the ruins had a sophisticated understanding of astronomy and celestial mechanics not seen before on Earth. They may have been wiped out by a great planetary catastrophe like an asteroid impact. However, their discoveries also attract dangerous attention. Mechanical sentinels destroy more of the ruins and attack the subs when energy pulses are emitted.

Through near-disasters and the edge of discovery, the crew begins to realize some greater unseen intelligence is actively monitoring and guarding the ruins site from humanity. Their exploration pulls back the curtain on aliens that once called Earth home, and unknown forces that now stir in the ocean's sunless depths. The story brings profound implications for life in the universe and mankind's understanding of the greatest frontier that remains - the oceans of our own planet.

**

About the Author

Mustafa A. Nejem is a maritime visionary with a captain's heart and an island soul. In his island home, the sea's love, sailing's legacy, and leadership's flame passed down through generations with pride and glory. He is a skilled navigator of words, charting a course through the vast ocean of knowledge. With his expertise and passion , he guide readers towards prosperous shores, unveiling the secrets of maritime life and business success in concise and captivating prose.